Radical Belonging

Radical Belonging

Stories of Love, Transformation, and Becoming

RITA SERGHINI

Bahía Books ☙ Palm Beach ☙ 2026

Radical Belonging: Stories of Love, Transformation, and Belonging

Published by Bahía Books
bahíabooks.com

For bulk purchases or for information on the author's speaking schedule, visit radicalbelongingbook.com

ISBN: 979-8-9952271-0-6 trade paperback
979-8-9952271-1-3 electronic book

Design and composition: Dick Margulis, dmargulis.com

For Marcela, my fiercest lesson of love,
and for every soul learning to belong

Contents

Preface

I DID NOT BEGIN THIS journey with the intention of writing a book. I began it as a mother trying to understand a world that did not know how to understand my daughter.

On the day Marcela was born, I was told she might not survive. If she did, they said, she would never walk or talk, never do the things a typical child her age might do. I listened, because listening felt like the responsible thing to do. I learned the language quickly—diagnoses, predictions, probabilities—words that promised clarity even as they quietly rearranged the future I hoped to claim. But Marcela has never belonged to the world of limitations, and over time I watched her move through and beyond the boundaries others tried to establish for her, not because she was exceptional, but because those boundaries were never as stable as they pretended to be. She spoke her first words at six months, walked at eleven months, and continues to break every boundary that has been established to define her.

Marcela did not arrive as a problem to be solved, even though the world often treats her that way. She arrived as herself, already expressive, already responsive, already significant. What no one told me was how much unlearning would be required or that she would become my greatest teacher. An educator of love, of justice, of identity, of what it means to be fully human in a world that is so often afraid of what it does not understand.

What surprised me most was not her resilience per se, but my own rupture. I was unprepared for how deeply my assumptions would be unsettled: by the medical predictions, the cultural narratives about disability, the quiet ways society would try to define her before she had the chance to define herself. And I was not prepared for the truths that kept emerging in the spaces between fear and love: that the world was wrong about her, that the world was wrong about disability, and that the world was profoundly wrong about what makes a life meaningful.

Marcela forced me, gently, insistently, sometimes through tears, to unlearn: to unlearn the idea of "normal"; to unlearn the hierarchy of minds over hearts; to unlearn that worth is something proven rather than something inherent. What I learned instead is this: the unknown invites uncertainty, especially around disability. But uncertainty is not a defect. It is a mirror held up to society that reflects back the values we carry, often without noticing, and the ways we decide who deserves love, dignity, access, and joy.

This book grew out of that unsettled space. It is the story of how I became myself through Marcela. It is also the story of how she became herself in a world that often feared, dismissed, or erased her. The stories that follow are not arranged as progress; they do not move toward mastery. They move through everyday moments on playgrounds and in classrooms, in doctors' offices, grocery stores, airplanes, and living rooms, moments where identity is quietly shaped through looks, comments, policies, and assumptions made with little thought. These micro interactions leave imprints on our hearts, and they teach us who we are allowed to be. My experiences move through the evolution of my understanding, through the science, the philosophy, the failures, the ruptures, and the reframings. The book is rooted in the science of emotion, belonging, and relational knowledge and the ways our hearts send more signals to our brains than our brains send back. It is about the deepest truth adversity taught me: we know the world through our hearts first, and our minds then follow.

Love here, in this book, is not a feeling or a reward. It as an intentional practice, a philosophy, a pedagogy, a leadership stance, a way of being in the world that is active and accountable. Love is the work of building belonging and of seeing each other fully.

Disability is not the subject of these pages so much as the lens through which my thinking was interrupted and reshaped. Some of these pages carry my voice; in others, Marcela speaks in her voice: clear, bold, humorous, fearless, vulnerable. She shares her truth without apology. She names the moments that hurt her and the moments that strengthened her. She names what she has endured and what she refuses to accept. It is also a story of how a teenage girl insisted on her right to be visible, brilliant, joyful, complicated, and whole in a world that too often tried to simplify or diminish her. Marcela does not soften her memories for your comfort or mine. She tells you what happened, how it felt, and who she became because of it. Most importantly, she names who she is becoming.

Together, our voices braid into a single truth: Disability is not the problem. Dehumanization is.

I write without conclusions because the life we are living has not offered me many. And yet, this is not a book of despair. What it offers instead is a different kind of attention, one that asks us to stay with what is unfinished, to learn through unlearning, and to resist the impulse to make meaning too quickly. If you are an educator, this book will ask you to consider the imprints you leave. If you are a parent, it will ask you to rethink your inherited ideas of "normal." If you are someone living with disability, may you feel seen here, not as a source of inspiration, although maybe that too, but definitely as fully human. And if you love someone who is different in any way, this book will show you how difference is not the obstacle. It is the doorway, an opening for understanding.

This is our story. It is messy and tender and brave. And it begins, as all true stories do, in the heart.

Acknowledgments

THIS BOOK WAS BORN in conversations and in quiet acts of trust.

Chloe and Leo, you are the quiet architecture beneath these accomplishments. Because of you, I grow. Because of you, I believe in the power of standing together.

Paco, my steady horizon. You love me within my intensity, and your constancy made courage possible.

Family, both born into and chosen through relationship, you gave my dreams a place to land.

To friends and educators whose long conversations and leisurely meals cultivated a sacred space for this book to breathe.

The cobblestone streets of Cádiz taught me community, and its widespread oceans invoked contemplation. Both live within these pages.

With gratitude to Joanie Eppinga of Eagle Eye Editing for her insightful editing and guidance, gently bringing together the many threads of this story.

If there is any wisdom here, it is because many hands and many hearts loved it into being.

The circular motif woven into this book comes from my husband's great-grandmother's needlework. She mended what was frayed and held together what might have unraveled, a reflection of strong love that sustains.

1

Premonition

My husband tells a story about the night before Marcela entered this world—a story he carried quietly for years before he shared it with me, and one whose meaning we still struggle to understand.

I was in the hospital, heavily pregnant, suspended in that strange in-between space where time slows and the world feels both close and far away. The monitors hummed their steady rhythms. Nurses moved in and out through the dim light. I was focused on staying calm, on the weight of anticipation, on the mystery of who I was about to meet and how I would meet her.

My husband tells me that in a moment of silence in that room, while I slept, he saw something: a vision, clear, vivid, and unmistakable. It still brings tears to his eyes all these years later to think of it. He says the Virgin Mary descended gently into the room and placed her hand on my stomach. It was not a gesture of warning, not a gesture of sorrow, but one of protection, of blessing, and of profound, almost unbearable tenderness.

For years we tried to interpret that moment. We asked ourselves questions that had no obvious answers: Was it a sign? A message? Foreshadowing? A preparation? We wondered whether it was meant to warn us, or guide us, or simply hold us through what we could not yet imagine. We spent countless late-night conversations circling the story like a flame, fascinated, humbled, unsure. Eventually, we stopped trying to decode it.

Because what stayed with us was not the why, but the knowing. Even then, even before she took her first breath, something in us understood what the world has often failed to see: that Marcela came into this life carrying a light that did not belong to ordinary things; that she would challenge us, break us open, and re-teach us how to see; that she was destined to move through the world differently, in a way that was not less, but deeper. Not fragile, but fierce. Not incomplete but overflowing with purpose.

Her path would not be smooth, and her difference would not be small. Her presence would not be quiet. She was meant, *intended*, for something more.

Looking back now, I realize that this moment was my first initiation into a new way of knowing. It was the beginning of my unlearning, a spiritual whisper revealing that motherhood would require intuition, humility, courage, and a radical openness to life's mysteries. It was the first sign that my daughter would be one of my greatest teachers.

And perhaps the Virgin's silent gesture, the hand placed gently over my womb, was not foretelling hardship but consecrating the love that would sustain us through it—a love fierce enough to withstand the world, and tender enough to transform it.

ෆ

People speak about the moment a woman becomes a mother as if it is a single instant, a clean, warm, cinematic transition. Mine was nothing of the sort.

Motherhood did not arrive with a soft glow or a perfect photograph. It entered through the side door, unexpected, uninvited, unfiltered. It came wrapped in fluorescent lights, clipped sentences, and the cold certainty of medical language. It came with rupture.

The story of Marcela's birth is not only the story of how she entered the world; it is the story of how I fell out of the woman I thought I was and into the woman I had no choice but to become. Some moments slice your world in half. They create a before and an after that can never be mended, because they were not intended to be. Marcela's birth was my rupture. There was a clear before, and an unmistakably different after.

The first thing I noticed was that the doctor didn't look me in the eyes when he spoke. His gaze hovered somewhere between my body and the tiled floor, as if the truth he was about to hand me was too heavy to carry face-to-face. "There are severe abnormalities," he said. "She may not survive."

I had just woken from an emergency C-section I never expected, my body still numb, my mind scrambling to catch up to a story that had already raced ahead without me. I asked my husband what the doctors had told him right after she was born, but he couldn't remember. Odd, because he remembers everything. Now I understand that sometimes memory softens itself to protect us from the sharpest edges. But nothing softened the weight of those words. The room felt unmoored, as though gravity itself had shifted.

And outside, the world echoed that shift. News had broken of a possible hurricane forming over Cádiz, something so rare it was almost mythical. People were bewildered. But deep within me, beneath language and logic, I understood. What I know now through lived experience, what I recognized then only as instinct: a cosmological shift was underway. She was coming, Marcela, and even before her first breath, she was rearranging the atmosphere. Sending waves. Signaling that nothing would remain the same, and telling us in her own way to brace for a different kind of storm.

A song played faintly on the radio, its title long forgotten, but its chorus repeated: *standing on shaky ground.* And oh, did I feel it. Not metaphorically, but physically, spiritually. Every part of me trembled at the knowing that the ground I had once trusted was no longer firm to stand on.

In that moment, all I could do was let go—of certainty, of timelines, of the story I thought I was living.

The possible hurricane outside and the undeniable hurricane inside my body converged, reshaping everything. And between those storms, a new truth formed: She had arrived already changing the world around her. Even before I held her, she was rewriting my life. She still is.

In the first hours of her life, before I fully knew her, before the world had the chance to impress itself onto her story, I felt something ancient rise in me: a kind of knowing that didn't come from logic or training or medical charts. Ancient because it felt like it belonged to a very distant civilization or past. It came from somewhere much deeper, somewhere more sacred. It came from the depth of my heart.

I knew she was meant to be here, that she was whole, that she was mine, not in the sense of ownership, but in the sense of becoming. And I knew that if she was going to fight for her life, as she had already done so fiercely to make it into the world, then I would fight for the world she was born into. The world wanted to hand me a narrative, one built long before Marcela's birth: a narrative of limits, of pity, of tragedy, of what disability "means." But the world's story didn't match what I was learning in the quiet hours between feedings and fear, between specialists and sleepless nights, between uncertainty and awe—what I was learning through my feeling and my heart.

The world defined disability as limitation. My heart defined it as humanity.

The world defined disability as deficit. My heart defined it as relationship.

The world defined disability as a medical problem. My heart defined it as a social mirror.

Something in me knew, even then, even without the language I have now, that if I accepted the world's story, I would betray her. I would betray myself. And I would betray the truth I felt pulsing in both of our chests. So, I made a decision: I would not let the world define her. I would let love define us both. Love not as softness, but as praxis—as the refusal to participate in her erasure, as the framework through which I would relearn what it means to be human.

ꕥ

For weeks after Marcela was born, I moved through life as if someone had turned up the saturation of the world. The birds sang louder, the clouds were fluffier, the colors of the leaves were brighter than I'd ever seen them. It was as if Marcela's presence sharpened my senses, as if by learning how to see her, really see how she saw, I was learning how to see the entire world anew. When I walked her through the neighborhood in her stroller, people stared. Their eyes lingered too long, too curiously, too unsoftly. I felt their gaze before I saw it. It carried a mix of confusion, pity, and something close to fear.

For a while, I internalized it. I felt exposed and vulnerable, as if those people's discomfort were a mirror reflecting something I had failed to protect my daughter from. But then something unexpected happened.

Marcela laughed. She laughed at the sunlight flickering through the trees. She laughed at a dog passing by or at the pigeon racing for food. She laughed because she was alive. Because life delighted her. And in her laugh, I heard a truth: She was not the one who needed protection from the world. Rather, the world needed protection from its own ignorance.

Marcela then, as she does now, triggers others. Her very existence mirrors to others what they are not capable of being. It reflects their lack of empathy and compassion, but instead of pausing to interrogate why or engage with what that reveals, people displace their discomfort onto her, mistaking their unease for her deficiency.

Marcela's disability was never a tragedy: It was a lens, a reframing, a call to consciousness. Every day with her was an opportunity to reevaluate what I thought I knew: about ability, identity, belonging, the body, and of course the heart. It is a lesson of learning that the heart is not merely an organ, but rather an instrument of knowledge, a key to unlock another way of knowing.

2

Rupture

WHAT I FELT FOR MARCELA wasn't just mother-love. It was an epistemic shift, a reorganization of understanding. It was as if her arrival rearranged the furniture of my soul.

Later, when I read Antonio Damasio's work on emotions and how gut feelings are somatic markers that unconsciously guide the foundation of decision-making, when I encountered the science showing that the heart sends more signals to the brain than the brain sends back, signals that influence emotions, decision-making, and mental states, then it all made sense. But that knowledge was to come years later. In the beginning, all I had was instinct, heart knowledge, a truth that you don't reason your way into but feel your way toward.

There is a particular silence that fills a hospital room when something is wrong, a silence that hums beneath the noise. Before anyone spoke, my body already knew.

Something inside me tightened, sharpened, and rose to attention. Mothers know, even when we are told nothing, even when the truth is being spoken around us, not to us. I watched faces before I heard words, felt the shift in the air that contained urgency without explanation, concern without language.

Then came the language: a diagnosis of a condition I had never encountered, leading to a future described as though it had already collapsed.

In that moment, I felt myself split—the woman I had been on one side, the mother I was becoming on the other. This is what unmaking feels like: a free fall with no promise of a landing.

ഗ

I did not see Marcela when she was born. Four days passed, four whole days, as they kept me in my room. To this day, I cannot piece together why. No one gave me a clear answer. The world kept moving, people kept whispering updates, nurses floated in and out, but my daughter existed only in photographs that others had taken. Everyone had seen her but me. On the morning of the fourth day, something in me snapped into clarity. I woke up, turned to my husband, and said, "Go find a wheelchair. I'm going to see Marcela."

He came back minutes later with a strange look on his face. He told me the nurse said I couldn't go downstairs because the wheelchair was old and "wouldn't hold me." That was the explanation. As if I needed the chair to hold me together, when the truth was that the only thing holding me at all was the need to get to my daughter.

I looked him dead in the eye and said, "Either you wheel me down or I will crawl down. But I'm going to see her right now."

He didn't say another word. He went back, grabbed the broken wheelchair, and wheeled me through those long, sterile corridors. My heart raced with a mixture of anger, anticipation, and the kind of grief that sits behind the ribs like a stone. I cried every time they showed me pictures of her—I was jealous, furious, aching. Why didn't anyone think it was important to bring her to me? Why did no one seem to understand that I needed her, that we needed each other?

When we reached her corner of the NICU, I felt the world narrow to a single point. Marcela was in an incubator, lying prone, her tiny body covered in wires and tape, machines blinking and beeping rhythmically around her. Her hair was shiny, almost red, like my hair. She was sucking on her finger, calm and determined, as if she had been waiting for me with more patience than I deserved.

Tears slid down my face. She was so small, so beautiful, so perfect. Overwhelming love flooded through me, love I didn't even know my body could hold.

A nurse approached and asked, almost puzzled, "Why are you crying? There is no need to cry." I remember turning toward her as if she were speaking from another planet. I had not seen my child for four days. Four days of distance I never agreed to. Four days my daughter was placed in the world without me. I felt it, deep and undeniable, that she had missed me as much as I had missed her.

The nurse helped me lift Marcela from the incubator and settle her in my arms. When my baby's body curled onto mine, something inside me clicked back into place. I sat in that chair for hours, not moving, barely breathing, memorizing her weight, her warmth, the rhythm of her tiny breaths. I only let go when they made me give her back.

Marcela spent 28 days in the NICU. And for 28 days, I sat in that same chair, holding her until someone told me I had to stop. And every day, when they told me to give her back, a piece of me stayed with her until I could return.

The NICU is a world with its own rules, a place where your baby is yours, but not fully. I entered that space carrying all the tools that had once defined me: competence, composure, obedience, trust in authority. I learned quickly that those tools were useless here.

Here, others made decisions about my daughter. They spoke of her as if they knew her more intimately than I did. But something in me began to rise, to say that this could not be the whole truth or the only story.

I was first introduced to the writings of bell hooks as a graduate student. I remember being taken aback by her insistence that love is not merely an emotion, but a transformative and ethical force, one capable of confronting and undoing systems of domination and oppression. Until then, I had understood love as something private and fleeting: a feeling, passerby, an individual experience untethered from justice or responsibility. The professor who introduced me to hooks spoke about human connection in ways that I had never contemplated, about the radical possibility that love could be used to recenter humanity and spirituality at the heart of justice work. This idea unsettled me. It asked something of me. It suggested that justice without love was incomplete, and that love itself demanded courage, accountability, and action. I read *All About Love* hungrily, and I was moved in ways that felt both profound and disorienting. I was inspired by this idea of love, but I did not imagine then that I, an ordinary person living an ordinary life, would come to experience what hooks was naming. That love could transform not only in soft, tender ways, but in ways that are powerful, fierce, and brave. That I would find a love that leaves such a mark. A love that, once felt, could never be unfelt.

ꕥ

While I was pregnant, I went to what felt like thousands of doctors. Each appointment came with its own set of measurements, its own opinions, its own theories about what they believed Marcela "had." Every specialist added a new layer of uncertainty, another diagnosis that wasn't quite a diagnosis. For months, I carried not only my daughter but also the crushing weight of prognosis after prognosis, referral after referral, each one weighing down on a body already doing the work of becoming. The fairytale of pregnancy promised by waiting hands and indulgences like pickles dipped in ice cream to satisfy whimsical cravings was not my pregnancy. There were no charming messages hidden in hunger, only exhaustion and the quiet unseen work of enduring.

In Suzy Welch's work, selfhood is not something discovered through detached analysis, but something clarified by sustained attentiveness to one's sense of self. Through the act of paying close, caring attention to who we are and how we move through the world. Welch suggests that becoming who one is meant to be requires witnessing: the ability to see oneself honestly and to be seen by others, particularly in moments of uncertainty. This kind of becoming depends on relational presence, the sort that invites people inward rather than holding them at a clinical or evaluative distance. It is in this space of care, attentiveness, and alignment that a more authentic sense of purpose begins to take shape. What I needed was not clinical certainty, but human presence. But here there was no invitation into relationship, no space to sit together inside the not knowing, only pronouncements and fear.

Not once did a doctor talk to me about becoming a mother. No one acknowledged the powerful connection I felt inside me, the raw, animal instinct to protect her, the tidal wave of love that made me want to move mountains just to clear a path for her tiny feet. Instead, the space between doctor and patient widened. I was met with cold, sterile phrases, delivered in fluorescent rooms by people who looked at charts instead of my face. No one talked about Marcela as a baby, a person with a life ahead of her, someone with gifts to bring into the world.

The further I moved into that pregnancy, the more it felt as though the medical world was studying my daughter while refusing to *see* her. Measurements, deviations, and risk percentages came at me like cold rain, but no one spoke to me about her as a child coming into the world with her own spirit, her own possibilities. Although bell hooks reminds us that love is a practice of recognition, an ethic of seeing one another with care, everything around me felt stripped of that love.

In a moment that still tightens my throat when I think of it, a doctor reduced my daughter to a phrase: "A child like this..." There was no recognition of her name, or her face, or her spirit, or the way her tiny hand curled around my finger. Just a phrase. A classification. I understood the violence of language, how a single sentence can shove a mother to the edge of herself. In that moment I felt what Sara Lawrence-Lightfoot teaches: that when people are reduced to fragments, their story becomes distorted. The portrait of my daughter was painted entirely by others, experts who saw abnormalities but not a baby, complications but not possibility. I had to reclaim her story. I had to reclaim my own. I decided then: I will not let this world tell my daughter who she is. And I will not let it tell me who I must be.

After a doctor's appointment. I got into my car and drove with no destination in mind, as though motion itself might outrun what I had just been told. The world outside looked unreal, blurred at the edges, as if I had been dropped into someone else's life. When I finally pulled over on the side of the road, my chest tightened, my hands shook, and a quiet, desolate stillness filled the car. For the first time in my life, I felt completely unmothered by the universe. And in that moment, for the first time in a long time, I prayed, a plea from the rawest place in me: "Please... please help her. Please help me survive this. Please don't let me lose her before I even get to love her."

And then something—God, the universe, my own deepest knowing—whispered back: "You will love her the way she needs to be loved. And she will love you into someone you have not yet become." It would be a love that required presence, a willingness to be affected by what I was seeing. A love that was willing to allow us to be together, allow me to be a mother already bound to a child through hope, fear, and fierce attachment.

In that moment on the side of the road, I understood: I wasn't being asked to be strong. I was being asked to be transformed.

3

The "Good Girl"

BEFORE MARCELA, BEFORE THE NICU lights, before I learned how fragile and constructed the world really was, I lived inside a story I didn't know I was telling myself.

This is the part of the story that is quiet but essential. Because when Marcela came into my life, she disrupted not only what I believed about disability and about adversity, but also what I believed about *myself.*

There are many ways we begin to comprehend the mysteries of life, how to engage soulfully in the beautifully complex experience of arriving in this world, living for a handful of extraordinary years, growing older and wiser, and eventually moving on from the known into the less known. I was born in the United States and raised in a middle-class family. I had everything I needed and much of what I wanted. And yet I always felt like a stranger there. The rhythm of the place never matched the rhythm inside me. I didn't understand the people, the way of life, or the quiet expectations that seemed to define "belonging." I carried far more questions than answers. Looking back now, I'm struck by how deeply I *knew*, even then. I didn't trust that inner knowing, but it was unmistakable: That place was not my place.

Growing up was awkward because something in me was consistently drawn elsewhere. It felt like a magnetic pull, subtle but steady, guiding me toward a path I could not yet see. From as early as I can remember, I yearned to explore the world I didn't know. I daydreamed about distant lands, unfamiliar languages, and ways of being that didn't resemble the world around me.

I used to stand in front of the mirror and pretend I was from somewhere else, speaking a language I had never learned yet somehow knew. I was fluent in my imagination, and that fluency made me feel powerful. Not knowing didn't make me uncomfortable; it made me feel alive. Those butterflies, the anticipation of stepping into the unknown, were my compass long before I understood what they were pointing toward.

Eventually, the fire inside me became too bright to ignore. I left first my city and then my country and moved across the ocean to Spain. Spain changed me in ways so profound I still search for adequate language. I knew nothing of her until I met her—and yet she welcomed me as her own. Spain taught me to unthink everything I thought I knew. That once-unfamiliar place became the soil I needed for the deepest questions of my life. It showed me how good loving life can feel. I learned what it means to feel good, to do good, to *be* good.

I had grown up learning how to be *good*. But it wasn't the same kind of good. It was really how to be agreeable, how to earn the approval of adults who rewarded neatness, discipline, and achievement. I learned early that being "easy," being "smart," being "helpful," made the world smoother, because it made me acceptable. Goodness from my upbringing was a currency, and I learned to spend it well.

I learned to read a room before I entered it. I learned to shrink the parts of myself that felt inconvenient. I learned to anticipate what people wanted and to deliver it flawlessly. I became fluent in a language many women know by heart: the dialect of performance, of pleasing, of becoming who others needed me to be.

Spain allowed me to question who I was raised to be. I used to ask myself, how could something so unfamiliar become so essential? How could a place I wasn't born in shape me so deeply in comparison to the place that raised me? I was intrinsically holding the tension between formation and becoming and questioning if belonging can be chosen rather than inherited. I was believing what I was taught while at the same time being pulled to follow something unteachable.

ᔓ

My father died when I was ten. He had immigrated to the United States on a Fulbright scholarship. As I grew older, I learned how to live with his absence, but I always carried a quiet knowing that, like him, I was destined for something different—another way of life, a place both distant and unfamiliar.

Spain gave me the courage to take that leap of faith. From there, I traveled into the unknown of Morocco to meet the family I had never known on my father's side. I used to write letters to my aunt, Zorah. I kept them simple. I assumed she did not speak English, so I wrote about the weather, reminded her of my age and grade, and offered small updates about my life. Year after year, I mailed a letter, marking the changes in my face and my becoming. She never wrote back, yet I continued.

I think I wanted her to see me, to witness my growth, to confirm that I was becoming something recognizable, something that might resemble my father. In writing to her, I realize now, I was not only searching for her. I was searching for myself.

I felt proud to do things others around me had not done. One morning, I woke up and decided I would take the ferry to Tangier and then travel on to Tétouan, the town where my father was born. I contacted my father's family and told them I was living nearby and wanted to meet them. His half-brother, Karim, agreed to meet me at the port in Tangier.

The seas were energetic, the crossing rough. Many people were seasick, but it did not bother me at all. I felt proud of that too, proud that I had grown up around water and boats, that my body knew how to steady itself. I sat in the sun, warmth on my face, wind pulling at my hair, filled with anticipation for what was coming.

The city was hot and dusty, marked by a kind of poverty I had never encountered before. It was my first time in a place like this, and as a woman, I felt anxious. People looked at me as though I were from another planet, or at least that is how it felt. Still, I refused to let that gaze penetrate my determination. I was told how to dress and how to behave as a female American.

The instruction startled me, but I wanted to respect the culture, so I complied. With every encounter, I was reminded of my privilege.

During the drive to Tétouan, Karim pulled over on the side of the road near a man with a camel. I remember thinking, why did he stop to show me a camel? It never occurred to me that he intended for me to ride it. Before I fully understood what was happening—I spoke no Arabic—I found myself being lifted onto its back. I had ridden horses before, but never a camel. They are enormous creatures, rising unevenly to stand, leaning forward to lift their back legs first, then rocking backward to straighten the front. Sitting atop it felt unreal. Me, on a camel, in Morocco. I could hardly believe it.

Morocco was alive with sound, with people, with unfamiliar smells and rhythms. Everything was different. Although I disliked the feeling of being on display, I was open to it all, thrilled by the adventure I had set into motion. I was the first of my siblings to come to this land, the first to meet this side of my family. It felt like an honor.

Many moments stayed with me: the mint tea, the men gathered outside street cafés, the markets humming with life. Once, I was invited to tour a pastry shop. As I walked through, people looked at me as if I were someone important, almost famous. Without a shared language, the exchange became entirely physical and generous. As I passed each station, employees pressed different pastries into my hands, one after another, until I was walking through the shop with my hands full, laughing, unable to refuse the sweetness being offered. Yet one memory reverberated more deeply than all the others. I was sitting on a bench in a town square lined with orange trees, just outside the house where my father had been born. It felt like a return, not only to a place but to an origin, as though time had folded in on itself and carried me back to the beginning of my lineage.

The Mediterranean sun warmed my entire body. My head felt hot, my shoulders softened, and my breathing slowed. In that warmth, something loosened. My mind, usually restless and searching, grew still. I was no longer trying to understand or explain; I was simply present. The questions Why me? Why here? did not disappear; but they softened, becoming less demands for answers and more invitations to listen.

In that quiet, I began to sense that learning does not always arrive through effort or instruction. Sometimes it emerges through attunement, through allowing the body to feel held by a place, by history, by something larger than oneself. Sitting there, I understood that I had not come to Morocco to solve a mystery or claim an inheritance, but to be witnessed by the land that had shaped my father, and to witness myself within it.

Later that day, I went to my grandmother's house for a family meal. I do not remember what the house looked like. It was dim, and there was too much to absorb at once. We removed our shoes at the door, and Karim guided me into the room where my grandmother sat waiting in a chair. In

Morocco, greetings are marked by three kisses on the cheek, rather than the two exchanged in Spain.

My grandmother was old and cautious. She wore black, an elderly elegance emanating from the only part of her I could truly see, her face. Her eyes were deep, holding both a life fully lived and the unmistakable weight of loss. I wondered if her sadness came from losing her son in another country and from never having the chance to say goodbye. Perhaps seeing him in me unsettled her. Perhaps my presence arrived too late to make sense of.

My aunt, though, needed no interpretation. Even though I could not understand her words, I felt an immediate and unmistakable connection to her. I had one memory of her from when my father was alive; she had visited us once in the United States. I remember almost nothing from that visit, only that she was there.

Without speaking, she took my hand and led me down a hallway to a closet. From a high shelf, she pulled down a box. Inside was a trifold wallet. When she opened it, every photograph I had ever sent her spilled out—year after year of my becoming, carefully saved. She looked at me, tears streaming down her face, and said one sentence in broken English: "I have waited all these years."

I was forever changed.

Foreignness, traveling, living, working, and eventually raising a family in a country that was "not mine" taught me something I could not yet articulate: that difference was not something I stumbled into, but something that had always been calling me. I began to wonder whether it was only geography, constructed by human hands, that had separated me from what my inner being already recognized as home. These experiences quietly taught me that belonging is not always conferred by borders, language, or permission. They invited me to trust a form of knowing that does not require external validation.

Long before I had the language for it, I was being prepared to question systems that confuse legitimacy with authority and sameness with safety. When institutions would later insist on definitions, diagnoses, and compliance, I already carried a truth they could not teach me: identity is not granted by systems, and belonging is not something earned by fitting in. I had learned, slowly and without instruction, that home is not always where you are allowed to be. Sometimes it is where your soul recognizes itself.

Ironically, or perhaps inevitably, in Cádiz—the Spanish town that took me in as its own—there is a saying: Un Gaditano nace donde le da la gana. A person from Cádiz is born wherever they choose. The phrase did not surprise me. It only named what I already knew.

❧

My work as an international educator deepened this understanding. Guiding students through the role of culture in self-discovery filled me not with certainty, but with recognition. I watched people grow, shift, and become more of who they longed to be—not who they had been trained to become.

I remember one student in particular, and although I cannot remember her name, I can still see her face clearly. Young, eager, and unsure. She ended up staying in my program for an additional term, not because she had to, but because something in her had been irrevocably altered by the experience of *elsewhere.*

One morning she came to my office and sat down with an almost ceremonial seriousness. I was surprised that she said that she wanted to talk about me. She asked me how I had gotten to where I was, how I had ended up with a life and a job like the one I had. It was her ideal life. I told her the truth: that it wasn't a linear plan so much as a series of permissions. That I had allowed myself to go places I had never been, loosened my grip on the scripts that told me who I was supposed to be, and trusted in myself in a way that each step, taken without full certainty, was guiding me toward something I believed was truer for me. I could see her absorbing my words, her eyes bright with the thought of possibility; and yet something in her remained weighted and unresolved.

So, I asked her what was really going on.

She began by telling me that her mother was an accountant. Her father was an accountant. And it was simply understood that she, too, would become an accountant. The problem, she said quietly, was that she did not want that life. She wanted the freedom to choose to decide who she was becoming. But that desire came with a burden: the fear of disappointing her parents, of stepping outside the expectations that had already been written for her. Her struggle was not a lack of ambition or discipline; it was the quiet violence of being asked to live a life that did not belong to her.

Over and over again, in ways that mirrored my own experience, I witnessed the same quiet awaking in my students. Coming to Spain and studying abroad created a rupture, a pause in the inherited momentum of their lives. It offered students a space where their identities were no longer pre-interpreted, where no one knew their history or expected them to perform a familiar role. In that space, they were invited to take the reins of their own learning, to make decisions fully, and to listen inwardly without their inner knowing being overridden by external demands.

Elsewhere gave them something rare: the chance to understand themselves. Before belonging to a profession, a family narrative, or a system of expectations, they were allowed, perhaps for the first time, to belong to themselves. To stop interrupting their own wholeness. And in that act of self-belonging, something essential came back online: agency, coherence, and the quiet courage required to live a life that feels like one's own.

In those moments, I felt part of something larger and unfinished. Education became more than a profession. It became a space where questions mattered more than answers, where becoming was allowed to remain in motion.

I did not yet know how deeply my own understanding of learning, belonging, and intuition would be challenged. I only knew that something in me was being prepared.

Spain did not know me.

That was its gift.

There, I was unaccompanied by my history, with no inherited roles, no accumulated explanations, no one to confirm who I had been. I was no one's memory, no one's shorthand. I moved through streets where my name carried no resonance, where my past had no grammar. And in that anonymity, something quiet but radical occurred: I became legible to myself.

When the external scripts fell away, I began to listen inwardly. Without fluency, linguistic, cultural, or emotional, I had to learn to pay attention differently. To gesture. To tone. To the body's knowing. Spain required me to live without guarantees: no promise of coherence, no witness to my becoming, no assurance that what I was building would last. And yet, it was there, precisely there, that I learned self-belonging must precede relational belonging.

Elsewhere is not merely a location; it is an exercise. It is what happens when you leave the life you were handed and step into one you can build yourself, brick by brick, without blueprints, without approval. Elsewhere teaches you how to stand without being held in place by familiarity. It asks: Who are you when no one is reminding you?

In Spain, I learned that identity is not something we perform for recognition but something we assemble through attention. I learned that belonging does not begin with being seen by others, but with seeing oneself clearly enough to stay with who one is. What I carried home was not a version of myself shaped by approval but one forged through presence. I did not return fluent, but rather, I returned aligned with myself.

There will come a moment when no one around you knows who you have been. Your history won't precede you. Your name does not carry explanation. The world will feel quiet in a way that is terrifying, but also clean. This will not feel like freedom at first. It will feel like erasure, but know this: it is initiation.

You will look for mirrors but find none. And so you will have to learn, to listen instead.

Listen to what rises when there are no scripts to follow. Listen to the body before language, to intuition before approval. Without fluency, without witnesses, without guarantees, you will learn to choose yourself, not loudly, not perfectly, but faithfully. This is where self-belonging is initiated. Do not mistake loneliness for failure. There is a difference between being unseen and being unheld. You are being asked to hold yourself.

There will be days where you will miss the life you were handed, not because it fit, but because it was known. Resist the temptation to rush back into familiarity, to earn recognition, to make yourself legible to others before you are legible to yourself. Resist it. Stay long enough to hear your own voice without interruption. Stay long enough to learn that you are real even when no one is watching because familiarity is not the same as belonging.

One day, you will understand that belonging is not something the world grants you, and it is not always warm or affirming. Belonging is something you practice, through attention, through courage, through the willingness to remain true to yourself when certainty dissolves. It asks you to live without applause.

If you feel scared, that means you are doing it right. If you feel untethered, it means you are building something new. Trust that what you are assembling, slowly, quietly, without applause will hold. Because you are already enough.

ᔓ

Looking back, I can see the scaffolding. School taught me that intelligence is measured, ranked, and validated by systems that reward conformity. Family taught me that strength meant endurance, not vulnerability. Culture taught me that belonging is earned by fitting into the right categories, the right expectations, the right silhouettes. Faith communities taught me that love is conditional, granted to the obedient, the grateful, the high-achieving. No one said these things aloud; they didn't have to. I absorbed them anyway.

I internalized the rules: Be productive. Be agreeable. Be exceptional. Be grateful. Do not disrupt. Do not question. Do not need too much.

This is how identity construction works: quietly, invisibly, until one day you believe the story is your own. But the truth is I was constructed. Like all of us. And like all constructions, I was vulnerable to collapse.

Years later, I learned that so was Marcela.

Long before Marcela had the words for it, I began to notice that she was already learning to doubt herself. She was learning to apologize for simply existing. She was learning anger at who she was and jealousy for who she was not.

She was only five the day I fully understood it. We were walking home from school, crossing the small plaza we crossed every afternoon. A group of older kids came toward us, loud, carefree, unbothered by the world. Something in Marcela shifted. Without thinking, she slipped behind my legs, her small fingers gripping the fabric of my pants as if the world required her to shrink.

She wasn't hiding because she was shy; she was hiding because she was already afraid of their gaze. And I realized, with a shock so sharp it took my breath, that she was learning, at five years old, that her body, her difference, her presence might invite judgment. She was already anticipating harm. She was already adjusting herself in response to what others might say or think. In that moment I saw clearly that the world had begun writing her story before she could write her own.

And the version they were offering her, the one shaped by ableist stares, whispered comments, and unspoken assumptions, was nothing like the story we told her at home. Theirs diminished her. Ours insisted on her brilliance, her wholeness, her rightful pride.

The contrast lodged deep inside me like a stone, inviting me to reconsider all that I had known and decide on a new path.

If you had asked me then who I was, I would have answered confidently: a strong woman! A leader, an academic, a problem-solver; someone who strives and overcomes, someone whose value is in what she does rather than who she is.

I didn't know that these definitions were brittle. I didn't know they were built from external validation rather than internal truth. I didn't know they would fail me the moment the lived experience shifted the world beneath my feet.

Because when Marcela arrived, none of these qualities mattered. In the NICU, I learned that no one cares if you are strong or accomplished. No one applauds your leadership skills or your carefully constructed identity. There is no performance in a room filled with beeping monitors. There is only humanity, raw, exposed, unadorned.

And mine felt suddenly unfamiliar. The days after Marcela's birth were a blur of uncertainty, medical terminology, and the unnerving sense that I was no longer in control of my own story. I felt the old scaffolding tremble. The "good girl" in me wanted to impress the medical team, to ask the right questions, to be the kind of mother they approved of. But the terrified mother in me wanted to scream, demand answers, reject the underlying message that something was *wrong* with my child.

I remember what it felt like, her first questions about cruelty. Marcela would tell me quietly, sometimes in tears, that she could remember every single hurtful thing people had said to her. "It's like it's carved inside me," she once said. And I knew she wasn't exaggerating. I could feel it too.

Science says the brain remembers pain to keep us alive, an evolutionary instinct, a vigilance against the lion hiding in the brush. Better to remember danger than beauty; survival depends on it. But what they don't always say is that the heart remembers, too. Marcela taught me that the heart wrinkles where it is bruised, the same way a wrinkled piece of paper stays creased no matter how gently you smooth it back out.

I used to do an activity when I taught about emotional harm: wrinkle the heart, insult it, apologize to it. It stays altered. Still whole, but permanently changed. Marcela carries those early wrinkles in her heart, and I knew that part of my work, my motherhood, my responsibility, was to help her learn how to live with them without letting them define her.

When I understood how deeply the heart shapes our sense of self, I had to confront who I wanted to be as her mother. I wanted to protect her, yes. But I also wanted to teach her how to move through injustice without losing the best parts of herself, her joy, her laughter, her unfiltered tenderness. I wanted her to know she was worthy, inherently, regardless of what anyone else believed. I wanted her to love herself more fiercely than the world could wound her; to trust her heart more than they feared her difference; to respond with integrity even when met with cruelty.

My two selves collided in those early days: the one I had been taught to be, and the one I was becoming.

Marcela's presence didn't break me—she broke the illusion, the impossible expectations I had accepted.

There are moments in life when something inside you rearranges itself so suddenly, so unmistakably, that you can feel it undeniably. For me, that moment arrived quietly. No thunder, no announcement, just a sharp interior click. A *knowing.* It was the moment I realized that becoming Marcela's mother required a shedding: of the identities I had inherited; the obedience I had been taught to perform; the unquestioned belief that systems know better than intuition, better than love, better than me.

Before Marcela, I moved through the world believing that expertise lived outside of me. But with her arrival, something shifted, an inner recalibration I didn't yet know how to name.

Only later did I realize that back in those early NICU days the shape of that shift was already revealing itself. A doctor spoke about Marcela in clinical terms so cold they barely grazed the edges of her humanity. He spoke of her future as though he were estimating the value of something replaceable. And suddenly, the clarity inside me sharpened. I realized that if *I* did not protect her story, someone else would write it for her. If *I* did not stand in the truth of who she was, her right to the freedom to become, the world would define her in ways that had nothing to do with her. And if I did not allow myself to become who I needed to be, I would remain small in a moment demanding I become vast.

So when the doctor pushed for immediate surgery—one she would likely not survive, by their own admission, having been performed five times before, with three of the children dying—the recommendation was offered with a startling casualness. The options were laid out as if they were neutral pathways rather than life-altering gambles, as if my child were a case to be managed rather than a person to be protected. There was even an option grounded less in knowledge than in uncertainty, presented with the same clinical ease. It was cold. Distant. As though experimentation were simply another form of care.

And in that moment, something ancient rose up in me—the kind of resolve bell hooks describes as love in action. Love not as sentiment, but as liberation. Love as the fierce refusal to surrender another's humanity to systems that mistake procedure for wisdom. When I said no, it was not rebellion. It was becoming.

They were stunned. No. One word. One choice.

My sister-in-law, Olga, still speaks of that moment with disbelief. She says she could never have gone against the advice of a medical professional. She tells me that the deep knowing I had with Marcela was always there, from the very beginning. At the time, it did not feel courageous. It felt inevitable. It was the only thing that made sense. I had no proof that my choice was the right one. In fact, for a moment, I doubted myself. I was afraid, terrified, of the consequences of choosing wrong. But then I realized something equally unsettling: they had no proof either. They could not protect her any more than I could. The difference was not certainty. It was proximity. I knew her. I felt her. I was accountable to her life, not to protocol.

What guided me was a deep ancestral pull, urging me to trust myself more than I trusted them. In that room, my child was being reduced to probabilities and outcomes, her body treated as something to act upon rather than someone to listen to. I could not consent to that erasure. Saying no was not a rejection of medicine, it was a refusal to allow my daughter to become an experiment in someone else's uncertainty.

Later, I found language for what had happened inside me. That identity is not inherited it is *crafted*. That becoming oneself requires an unlearning, a reorientation toward the values and truths that originate from within one. And that is exactly what Marcela's life had initiated in me: the architecture of a new self, built not from obedience, but from clarity, intuition and love. One that originated from within.

Marcela was never a detour in my life. She was my blueprint, a call back to my *knowing*: the unmaking of the woman I was and the beginning of the woman I was always meant to become.

ᔕ

Once I began reading *Siddhartha*, I could not put it down; in fact, I did not move until I finished the entire book. The philosophical and spiritual themes exploring life's essence and humanity's interconnectedness resonated deeply. The paradoxes between good and evil, perfect and imperfect, emptiness and fullness were profoundly clear, as was the conviction that both halves are needed to form the whole. I was especially moved by the idea that knowledge gained through teaching does not equate to wisdom truly learned. Siddhartha's lesson, that peace comes from within, through spiritual experience, disciplined practice, and selflessness, is an urgent message for all of us.

The parallels between Siddhartha's journey and mine revealed themselves easily. Studying leadership taught me that leading requires service and sacrifice; we can choose to respond to life with purpose and meaning, and in doing so, we create opportunities to stretch our capabilities and become more than what we are. Choice is inherently human, but we also bear the responsibility to choose actions that deepen our impact. But how do we make the best choice? Marcela taught me that when we listen with the heart, we listen entirely and completely, absorbed by it, with eyes closed. I was reminded again, by God, the universe, and life, about the importance of listening.

∽

In 2016 I was diagnosed with an aggressive malignant tumor. The shock reverberated through every ounce of my body, heart, and soul. I realized in an instant that I had not been living as purposefully as I could have and that now I might not have the chance to.

I had three small children at the time. My son was only three, my middle child four, and Marcela was seven. Everything in my life suddenly contracted into a single point of fear, clarity, and urgency. As the doctor discussed my needing immediate surgery, his words struck me: "Sometimes these things happen to slap you in the face and tell you to wake up." I will never forget the way he said it: matter-of-factly, almost gently, and yet it was shattering. What had I been waiting for?

After the surgery, my oncologist told me that the tumor had come within 0.8 mm of breaking through, of spreading, of metastasis. In his words, I was "within 0.8 mm of having a completely different life experience," including chemotherapy, long-term treatment, or worse. That fraction of a millimeter became, for me, the distance between the life I had been living and the life I was being asked to claim.

In that moment of ultimate vulnerability and utter brokenness, I was given an opportunity to wake up. I finally listened to what life had been trying to tell me, and two messages emerged with startling clarity. First, that great love can emerge through suffering. I can say with complete honesty that out of my darkness came the brightest of lights, one that filled me with a love so strong it became life-altering. Second, that it was time to redirect my focus: to stop worrying about doing something and learn to move through life by feeling meaning and purpose.

Because of that 0.8 mm, I am a different person. My search is no longer rooted in goals and gains, but in the conviction that when all is said and done, I want to have made a meaningful contribution, to fulfill my potential and become that change I want to see in the world. And I am fortunate enough to have been given the gift of time so that I can pursue this more fully. And to have my daughter, tiny, fierce, impossibly alive, as my guide.

4

Systems That Teach Us to Doubt

I DID NOT BECOME A MOTHER the day Marcela was born. I became a mother the day I refused to remain the woman the world expected me to be. That unmaking saved us both. I remember a doctor standing at Marcela's incubator, speaking about her oxygen levels and brain scans while I was still reeling from childbirth. I remember the clinical tone used to describe her body, not cruel, but insensitive, simply... detached. As if detachment were a virtue. As if love were irrelevant.

I had entered motherhood as someone who had spent years in higher education. I had been shaped by hierarchy, institutional norms, the worship of expertise. Academia had taught me to trust what is cited, published, validated, and externally verified. It had taught me to view knowledge as something that lives outside the body. So when the medical professionals spoke, I deferred, even when something in my chest screamed *No, that's not who she is*—even when I felt the truth of her body on my chest, pulsing and warm and human, contradicting the predictions of development charts.

There are institutions that promise clarity. Hospitals. Universities. Clinics. Classrooms. They claim to offer evidence, expertise, diagnosis, and meaning. They speak the language of certainty. But when Marcela arrived, these systems did not offer clarity: They offered a verdict.

And I, a mother, scholar, woman trained to trust expertise, felt my own identity slip quietly into the background. I became the person standing next to the monitor, next to the chart, next to the "objective truths" being spoken *about* my child, but never *with* us in mind.

In faculty meetings, we spoke about equity and inclusion. In the NICU, I asked permission to hold my own child. And slowly, something started to unravel inside, not like the corrective unraveling of inherited identities that I previously felt, not the moral shattering, but a quieter fracture: the fracture between who I was in the world and who I was allowed to be as Marcela's mother.

When a nurse said, "Be careful, moms sometimes interfere with the lines," I apologized. When a doctor gave me the names of specialists to contact, I nodded. I brought my degrees, my publications, my professional identity into that room—but none of it mattered.

The systems that trained me to question everything had, ironically, made it harder for me to question *them*. It is a strange thing to realize that the institutions you once believed in were never designed with you, or your child, in mind. The NICU was not designed for a mother to learn her child—only to learn compliance. Higher education was not designed for a mother to trust her intuition—only to trust methodologies. I lived suspended between two systems that claimed ownership of truth. And yet, in both spaces, hospital and university, I felt the same thing: The more expert they sounded, the smaller I became. There was one moment, seemingly small, when the spell began to break. A nurse placed Marcela in my arms and said softly, "Just hold her. She needs you . . . but you cannot take her home."

Twenty-eight days after her birth, I woke with a certainty I couldn't explain: Today was the day we would be taking Marcela home. I had packed her tiny bag, slipped in the "first day out of the hospital" outfit I'd been saving, and told my husband, Paco, "Let's go. She's ready—I can feel it."

When we arrived at the NICU, I couldn't run, so I speed-walked through the hallway toward her area. Marcela was no longer in the most intensive part of the unit; fewer wires, fewer alarms, more baby than patient. She was drinking small bottles, oxygenating well, making soft newborn sounds that felt like sunlight after a long storm. I sent Paco to find the doctor in charge to start the discharge paperwork. He went off smiling, light on his feet for the first time in weeks. While he was gone, I fed Marcela, changed her, and dressed her in her little outfit. It felt like a ritual, a claiming. Then I saw Paco walking back toward me, his face wet with disappointment. "What happened?" I asked.

"Simon, the doctor in charge, says she can't go home today," he said quietly. "Something about feeding her . . . I don't know."

I felt a calm come over me, the kind of calm that precedes clarity. It did not feel like hope or denial, but like knowing. There was no argument forming in my mind, no list of reasons I was preparing to defend. It was simply there, steady, grounded, immovable. "Finish dressing her," I told him. "I'll go talk to him."

I walked to Simon's office and told him we wanted to take Marcela home. He shook his head. "It's not a good idea. She feeds slowly. She could dehydrate. It takes a lot of time to care for her."

"I have all the time in the world," I said. "Who better than her mother?"

"She'll need feeding every couple of hours," he insisted.

"And who better than I to do that?" I repeated. "In here, nurses have several babies to care for at once. At home, she will have me all to herself." He paused, then said she might be ready in a couple of days. It wasn't that he didn't care, I believe he did. But he could not feel what I felt: Marcela alone inside a hospital, us alone outside of it, a family split apart in a moment when we needed to be one.

Maya Angelou writes about feelings of freedom and oppression, between those who move through the world unencumbered and those who must navigate it through watchful eyes. She does not romanticize suffering, nor does she deny its weight. Instead, she shows how people endure, how they overcome not through isolation, but through connection, through family, through the strength of one's sense of self. She explains that survival is communal, inherited, and sustained through love, memory, and voice. She reminds us that even within systems designed to confine, there are spaces of resistance, found in kinship, in belonging, and in the refusal to be erased.

I knew that our souls were entwined, that we were journeying through the world together, with intention and purpose, and that he could not understand because he hadn't lived it. When Simon told me that I could not take her home, his voice carried the authority of the institution, the confidence of protocol, the weight of expertise. And yet, as he spoke, something in me refused to shrink. Something inside me whispered, quietly but unmistakably, *You know something he doesn't.*

"Simon," I said, "you're not hearing me. I'm not asking for permission to take my daughter home. I'm telling you I'm taking her home today. Please prepare her discharge papers." There was nothing left for him to say but okay.

As I walked back toward Paco, I felt a deep sense of alignment, of stepping into the woman I was meant to be. "We're taking her home," I exclaimed to him. His whole face broke open in disbelief and joy. We hugged, gathered our tiny daughter, and walked out of the NICU doors, hoping never to return.

5

Radical Belonging

THROUGH MY RESEARCH, I FOUND what I had already begun to learn through motherhood: Identity constructed through disability invites deeper critical reflection. Participants reflected on paradox, tension, absence, relationality, intersectionality, and heart change, patterns supported by developmental theory but shaped most powerfully by our own lived experience. What disability reveals is a kind of cognitive stretching— reorientation toward the self that refuses simplicity, a way of navigating life that is built through contradiction, complexity, and resilience.

In a 2025 presentation, I described disability as an epistemology of going beyond simple survival to being able to thrive through creativity, as a way of gathering knowledge from lived struggle, embodied difference, and the constant negotiation of a world that was not designed for you. It is a way of making sense that is honest, emotional, imaginative, and whole—all the things academia has been trained to resist. It is precisely this complexity that gives disability its transformative power. In higher education, knowledge about disability has been historically constructed from the outside, through scrutiny, pathology, and pity.

I stand firmly in the belief that *story*—my story, Marcela's story, the stories of disabled participants in my research—provides a depth of insight that theories alone cannot reach. When story and science are braided together, the disability experience shifts from deficit to depth.

Marcela was nine when she first stood on a stage and told the truth of her life out loud. What began as one story, one moment of courage, became the doorway to something neither of us had imagined: a platform for restorative justice, built from clarity, insight, and a radical commitment to her own human dignity.

The origin of her advocacy, and mine, is rooted in a moment of shared vulnerability.

Marcela had just recovered from a life-altering surgery—one that required her to wear large metal correctors externally on her leg to protect a bone that had been delicately separated and carefully realigned. When she was finally well enough to leave the hospital, we decided to go to the local zoo in Seattle.

That zoo was magnificent. Every animal imaginable, winding pathways through the trees and natural habitat, rides, cotton candy, everything designed to transport children and their families somewhere joyful, somewhere other than where they had been. As we wheeled Marcela through the park, I noticed people watching her. Their eyes lingered not on her face, but on the blanket draped across her legs and on what it concealed. I looked at her, expecting delight, a smile sparked by the wonder around us. Instead, her eyes were full, her face tense, as if she were holding something back. I asked her what was wrong. "Mommy," she said, "look how they all stare at me. I wish they wouldn't look at me and would just say hi." In that moment, something sparked inside me.

She was right. She was worthy of being seen, but not in the way she was being looked at. She deserved to be seen for what she had just endured. A twelve-hour surgery. Bones separated. Metal fixed to her body so she could heal. I thought, *If they only knew what she had overcome, they would roll out the red carpet. They would make sure she was first in line. They would want her to feel joy.*

The next day, I went to University Village, a large shopping center near the local university. I wandered into a small T-shirt design store, and as clearly as I have ever felt guided by something larger than myself, I saw the sign: DESIGN YOUR T-SHIRTS HERE. Marcela's words from the zoo still weighed heavily on my heart. I walked in and asked if I could make five shirts with a simple message: *Just Say Hi.* I explained why. The clerk listened quietly, visibly moved, and gave me a discount without my asking.

At the time, we were staying at the Ronald McDonald House. Marcela's surgery and recovery required a three-month stay, and that house became our refuge, a place that keeps families together when everything else feels fragile and life is falling apart. I gave Marcela the shirts, and she smiled brightly. We wore them together. People in the house noticed our message and talked to us about it. The consensus was that the shirts were cool and a creative idea to call for kindness.

When Marcela was finally well enough to travel we packed our bags, said our goodbyes, put on our Just Say Hi shirts, and headed to the airport to return to Spain. We thought it would be fun to arrive together in our matching shirts. What we did not anticipate is that anyone along the way would pay notice. I will never forget sitting in the VIP lounge at the Dallas airport, Marcela was in her wheelchair seated at a table with her siblings eating snacks. Paco and I were sitting at another table just behind them. We watched a man approach Marcela. He knelt down in front of her, meeting her at eye level, and began asking about her herself. Marcela talked with him easily. As I watched, I felt it, a kind of connective glow between them. Not spectacle. Not pity. But empathy. Transformation. Humanity. By kneeling, by listening, by allowing himself to receive her story, that man created space for something sacred. Marcela opened. Love flowed outward. And he, in turn, was changed by what she offered. It was then that I understood the true power of our experience. We could create relationship through difference. We could re-center human interaction around empathy and compassion. We could insist on seeing one another fully and, in doing so, have a chance of making the world a little more humane.

She had already begun giving talks—standing in front of crowds that would have once swallowed her—not because it was easy, but because silence had come heavier. In her very first talk, she named the hurts she carried. She named how strangers stared at her, pointed at her, whispered about her as though she could not see or hear, as though her humanity were somehow muted by her size. She described how it felt to walk into a room and feel the shift before she even looked up, the subtle nudges, the elbow taps, the widening eyes, the quick-but-not-quick-enough glances that always found her.

She once said, "When people stare at me, it hurts deeply, as if there was something wrong with the way I was born. I cannot help how I was born; I can only live the life I was given."

Her voice, steady and sincere, moved the room. In a few short sentences, she turned curiosity into accountability and accountability into possibility. And that moment became the spark for something much larger.

From that day on, she began to speak everywhere that invited her: at schools, universities, and organizations, and on radio and television. Her message was clear: *How we engage with one another matters. How we see people matters. How we speak to and about people matters.*

Everywhere she went, she told her truth with astonishing gentleness and precision. She called out what hurt her, not to shame people, but to help them understand. She explained what it feels like to be stared at, pointed at, or treated like an object of curiosity instead of a full human being. She described the aching confusion of being talked *about* instead of talked *to*.

She taught adults things they should have already known. And somehow, she did it without bitterness. What she wanted—what she still wants—is *change*. Change that restores dignity, not just for her, but for everyone.

Marcela taught me that courage is a practice, not a trait. I have read every book Brené Brown has written; she inspires me. She writes about rumbling in the ring and doing the work while others are simple spectators. She writes that courage is a habit, a way of being, learned through repeated acts of choosing vulnerability over avoidance. She teaches that vulnerability is the origin of belonging and love. We were in the ring, doing the work. We didn't become courageous in one moment. We became courageous through many moments of struggle and vulnerability: when strangers stared at Marcela, when systems resisted and we persisted. Instead of being something I reached for, courage became something I lived inside.

I will never forget the day the school director in Spain pulled me aside. She was gentle, well-meaning, certain in the way people often are when they've never had to fight for someone's humanity. She said, "You realize you will not be able to change everyone."

I simply said, calmly and without hesitation, "But can you understand why I have to try?"

Because by then, trying wasn't optional. Trying was who I was now. And standing there, I realized that advocacy is not measured by the number of minds changed. It is measured by fidelity to the truth you carry; by the refusal to shrink; by showing up, again and again, because your child deserves a world that sees her fully.

And part of my trying was that I, her mother, stood in awe, watching her build the kind of world she deserves to live in, one conversation at a time.

6

Heart Change

In my life, heart change entered through rupture, through the shock of Marcela's birth, through the NICU lights, through the language of risk that clung to her tiny body. It entered through fear, through grief, through a love so intense it startled me.

I used to believe I was already formed. I had degrees, experience, confidence, a stable understanding of myself. I believed I knew what motherhood would be. I imagined a smooth transition, a coherent identity, a predictable life.

But Marcela dissolved all of that. The dissonance of our medical experiences, the "uncertainty of her health," the sudden presence of disability in our family system stripped away the stories I had inherited about normalcy and what a "good mother" looks like. I had to confront the ableism I didn't know I carried. I had to sit with the grief of lost expectations and the guilt of admitting that grief even existed. I had to learn to ask: What if disability is not a problem but a portal?

I often think about the world my daughter was born into and the world she is helping me create. Between those two worlds lies a fault line, a quiet but undeniable tension between inheritance and imagination. We inherit systems, definitions, and expectations that shape who we are allowed to become. But imagination breaks that inheritance open. It asks: *What if the world were different? What if we could build something truer? Something that felt like coherence, alignment and fine-tuned-ness?*

The world I inherited told me to privilege expertise over experience. The world I imagine honors them both.

Living at this intersection, between what is and what could be, has reshaped my identity as a mother, a scholar, and a practitioner in higher education. It has also reconfigured my understanding of power. Power lives inside systems, yes, but it also lives in narratives. Systems are built on the stories we believe about each other. Change the story, and the system begins to shift.

I came to understand that people with disabilities intuitively understand this landscape because they live with systems that constantly misread them. They learn early to negotiate paradox: *I am seen and unseen. I am included and excluded. I am visible and invisible.* They live in tension and yet find ways to weave that tension into coherence. They develop identity not by following stages but by navigating contradictions.

This kind of navigation is its own form of intellectual labor. Its own kind of resilience. And yet, the world we inherited rarely acknowledges it, because we lack the necessary courage.

In higher education, this courage means redesigning systems that were never built with disabled bodies or minds in mind. It means shifting from compliance-driven access to human-centered belonging. It means rewriting curricula so students can see themselves, fully, not partially, reflected in the material. It means elevating silenced voices from the margin to the center of knowledge production.

In my own practice, it means telling the truth: that disability is not a problem to solve but a perspective to learn from.

The world we inherited has limitations. But imagination expands the map. Through Marcela, through my research participants, through my years in the academy, I have learned that the most transformative knowledge is born at the intersection of lived experience and structural critique. And disability, perhaps more than any other identity, reveals the gap between what the world claims to value and what it actually supports.

The world we imagine is always calling. And little by little, story by story, we are building it into being.

7

Learning to See Differently

THERE IS A MOMENT IN every journey when the world quietly shifts. It is rarely dramatic. It rarely announces itself. Instead, something subtle—an encounter, a question, a realization—interrupts your familiar ways of perceiving and forces you to look again. My daughter has been that interruption a thousand times over.

Before Marcela, I lived in a comfortable intellectual milieu that did not require me to question my assumptions about the world. Difference and raising a child with a disability interrupted that comfort.

This is where my real education began. I learned carrying Marcela into buildings without ramps. I learned sitting in meetings where people spoke about "people like her" as if she were data. I learned in the language of "accommodations," that the burden is placed on the individual to adapt, never on the system to transform.

Disability exposes the architecture of exclusion—not only the physical barriers but also the psychological and cultural structures that determine who is welcomed and who is merely tolerated. For years, the world asked my daughter to bend herself around systems. Eventually, I began asking why the systems weren't bending toward her.

My training as a scholar taught me to analyze, categorize, diagnose, and interpret. But raising a child with a disability demanded something different: humility. I realized that my expertise, rooted in dominant knowledge systems, had limits. What disability revealed, painfully and beautifully, was that expertise without relationship becomes a form of erasure.

This realization forced me to shift my pedagogy, both as a mother and as an educator. I began relying less on mastery and more on lived experience. The world looks different when you stop viewing otherness as deviation and start viewing it as knowledge.

Another thing I've learned is that identity is relational. We become through one another. Our sense of self is sculpted in the presence of others, especially in those relationships that demand authenticity, vulnerability, and deep care.

Disability accelerates this kind of relational development. People with disabilities often grow up negotiating their identity against the dominant narrative, learning to trust themselves over a world that frequently misunderstands them. This negotiation cultivates self-awareness, empathy, boundary-setting, and emotional intelligence far earlier and far deeper than most people realize.

As I listened more to people with disabilities, I saw the same pattern I saw in my daughter: a keen understanding of tension, contradiction, paradox, and relational truth in their lived experiences. While they were constructing identities, they were also constructing meaning. It made me question why their wisdom remains marginalized.

Once you see the world through the lens of Marcela, you cannot unsee it. You start noticing the ways institutions flatten human richness. You notice how often we prioritize efficiency over humanity. You see how systems define success in narrow, exclusionary ways. You begin to recognize ableism not only as a social bias but as a worldview, a way of organizing society around the illusion of independence, productivity, and the "ideal" body and mind.

Learning to see differently became my form of resistance.

But it also became an act of love. Because love is not passive. Love pays attention. Love notices what others overlook. Love chooses to see deeply, even when the world prefers shallow interpretations.

As I allowed Marcela and her disability to reshape my vision, my life reorganized itself around what mattered: presence rather than productivity, relationship over hierarchy, and meaning over measurement. My teaching changed, as did my scholarship and my parenting. I realized that disability also altered the way I saw myself. It asked me to expand, soften, and question. It asked me to integrate new layers of identity: mother, advocate, scholar of belonging, witness to resilience, steward of story.

To my surprise, I found that disability didn't make my life smaller—it made my vision wider. And something else magical happened. I had seen it before, briefly, peeking in and out across moments and experiences, but this time it revealed itself more clearly.

Disability or, more precisely, the way disability is misrepresented and misunderstood not only shaped Marcela, the person living with it. It did not only shape me as her mother. It became a family curriculum, one that shaped all of us. When Marcela was excluded so were her siblings. When she was misunderstood, the shock waves moved through our entire family system.

I have always felt that our family exists as more than people bound together in a single moment in time. When Marcela was little, I used to thank her for choosing me as her mother. She would always respond, "No, Mommy—thank *you* for choosing me to be your daughter." At the time, I did not know why this exchange felt so natural, so necessary. It was instinctual, almost reflexive. Only later did I come to understand it as a kind of ever-present knowing, something ancestral, rising from within, pulling me toward a shared journey that did not begin with us and would not end here either.

I believe our souls are traveling together through this life but also across time, across histories and dimensions we may never fully name. I believe we chose one another. We chose this life together in order to interrogate inherited notions of family, to question systems and institutions, to bring difference into the world not as deficit, but as inquiry. Not as something to be fixed, but as something to be understood.

This knowing revealed itself through my other children as well.

During one presentation Marcela and I gave, we opened the floor to questions. Chloe was in the audience. Someone asked her what it felt like to be the sibling of a person with a disability, and how she handled it. Chloe answered by telling a story, not about hardship but about scrutiny. She described how her friends did not merely say our family was "weird." They evaluated it. They assessed its legitimacy, as though it were their right to decide what counted as normal or acceptable.

Her father was from another country and was still learning English. Her mother spoke English but was learning Spanish. Her brother had red hair when no one else in the family did. She was the younger sibling, yet the largest in size, while the oldest sibling was the smallest. To many, these differences appeared strange. To Chloe, they were simply facts of our lives.

She said, with remarkable clarity, that if that was weird, then yes, we were weird. But then she paused and named something else entirely. What felt truly strange to her, she said, was the idea that everyone was supposed to be the same. She asked plainly, without apology, "Why can't we just accept and normalize difference and move on?"

The room erupted in applause. I felt it in my body—goosebumps rising on my arms. Chloe was twelve years old.

In that moment, it became unmistakably clear to me that exclusion never isolates itself to a single person. It reverberates outward, shaping siblings, families, communities—teaching children early who is permitted to belong and who must explain themselves. Difference does not wound on its own. What wounds is the demand to justify it.

And there, in my daughter's unguarded clarity, I saw again what Marcela had been teaching me all along: that difference is not the problem. Our resistance to it is.

8

The Night My Daughter Was Cropped Out

I DIDN'T KNOW THE MIDPOINT of this story, our story, would come on an ordinary Friday night in a school gymnasium filled with folding chairs, nervous students, and the faint smell of perfume and a shiny gym floor. I had walked into the Honor Society Induction ceremony at my children's school with the secret, naïve hope that this would be one of those rare evenings when otherness wouldn't be the main character, that my daughter could simply be a student, a peer, and a teenager.

But life—and society—have a way of reminding you when you have hoped for too much.

Two years earlier, we had uprooted our lives in Spain, crossed an ocean, and returned to the country where I was born and raised, because Marcela could get better care there, and all three children would have stronger educational opportunities. I also believed the social fabric was more expansive, more accepting. I came back to the U.S. believing I was giving them something better.

I had no idea that the moment that shattered that belief would arrive not in a hospital, not in a specialist's office, but under bright fluorescent lights shining on the gym floor.

That night, both my daughters were inducted in the National Honor Society, but only one of my daughters was actually welcomed and accepted. My first daughter, my miracle child, my defier of odds, my teacher of things I once had no language for, was placed in the back corner of the room as if she were an afterthought. My other daughter, Chloe, was placed with her classmates at the front few rows of the room. My husband, my son, and I sat in the bleachers watching adults shuffle awkwardly around Marcela's wheelchair, unsure of what to do with her body, her presence, her right to be fully seen.

We watched her classmates form a line, link arms, giggle, and pose for photos; we watched the adults direct everyone into their positions—everyone except my daughter.

The moment that pierced me wasn't even the inaccessible stage, or the command for all inductees to stand when not all were able, or the way Marcela's view was blocked by them when they did. It wasn't the awkwardness or the silence or the lack of anticipation concerning her needs. Those things were painful, yes. Familiar, yes. But the rupture came later, when the group picture was posted online and I realized that my daughter—who had rolled forward with courage, who had asked nothing but to be included—had been cropped out. Removed, as if she were a distraction or an inconvenience.

I was furious, but beneath the fury was something sharper: grief. And yet, as happens in these moments of rupture, something else rose with it.

Marcela's siblings were devastated. They couldn't make sense of it. My son, Leo, in dismay at the visible exclusion, attempted to go down to the gym floor and push her himself. He kept asking: *Why would they put her in the back? Why would they leave her out? Why do they act like this?* Their heartbreak pushed me toward a truth I had long known but hadn't faced fully: Disability isn't just Marcela's experience. It is ours, as a family and as a society.

I sat down the next morning and wrote. Not from anger but from a kind of sacred responsibility. I wrote as a mother, as an educator, as someone who has spent years researching belonging and inclusion, and as a woman who refuses to let her daughter, or any child, become collateral damage of someone else's discomfort. I told them who Marcela was and what she had survived. I told them how deeply she had fought to be there, and about the many times she had stared hardship in the face and returned with more courage than any of us. I told them the truth that society keeps trying to avoid: What hurts isn't the disability. What hurts is the exclusion, the being unseen.

And I invited them, genuinely, openly, to do better. To lead with empathy. To rise into the values they preach and to become a community capable of seeing every child's humanity.

But most of all, I wrote because I had to make meaning of the moment that broke me open. Midpoints do that. They don't tie things together; they tear things apart. They ask: Who are you *now*? Who will you become?

That night forced me to confront the difference between access and belonging, between being invited and being valued. And yet, even in that painful moment, there was light: the girl in the red dress. The one who stepped forward when everyone else froze, the one who pushed Marcela toward the group picture, even though Marcela could not be wheeled onto the stage; that girl did not leave Marcela behind.

One child—one act of courage—reframed everything. It reminded me that the work of belonging is never wasted, that love always has witnesses, and that even when institutions falter, individuals can rise.

This was the moment I began writing again, our book, that I had placed in the back of my mind, and the back of the bookshelf, for the last several months, not just for Marcela, but *through* her. The moment I understood that her life was not a series of hardships to endure, but a lens that revealed who we are and who we needed to continue to become.

This was the night I realized that radical belonging isn't an outcome. It's a fight, a practice, and a calling. It's also a way of mothering, a way of teaching, a way of living.

And this, right here, is where the book turns.

A few days later, the school replied.

Their message was long, careful, and earnestly written, I believe, with the best of intentions. It opened with an apology for missing my call and a reminder of their collective dedication to all students. The administrator writing to me explained her background: former academic support coordinator, a teacher for seven years in ESE classrooms, with a master's degree in special education. She wanted me to know her heart, her experience, and her intention.

She explained that the stage had been added at the last minute. They had planned for a female officer to escort Marcela and had chosen the seating arrangement not to exclude her, but because it was "an easy swap" from where she would have been if she were able-bodied. She said that asking all inductees to stand was "tradition" and that keeping everyone seated would have been "more awkward." She assured me that they had had students with temporary injuries before and had "always done our best."

When she wrote about the group picture, she clarified that she and another teacher had been crouching in the back holding candles and therefore could not see where Marcela ended up. They had reflected on what had gone well and what they would improve. They hoped the year ahead would be a positive one.

She stated repeatedly that they did not want Marcela to "stand out." They believed they were being careful, thoughtful, and responsible in a way that protected her. Because they had meant well, they had not looked at the impact of how things played out. And even though they had responded to my letter with carefully selected words, they subsequently posted the picture of the event on Facebook and intentionally cropped Marcela out of the picture, I can only assume, because they now saw what they had not before.

And this—this precise tension between intention and impact, between inclusion and invisibility, between not wanting a child to stand out and ensuring they belong—that is the core of the story I am telling.

Reading their response, I felt a recognition bubble up inside me: that we live in a world where people are so afraid of difference that they would rather make disability invisible than integrated. In trying to avoid singling Marcela out, they had erased her. In trying to protect her, they had diminished her. In trying to be careful, they had caused harm.

But their letter also revealed something else, something tender: They truly did not know. And I knew that you cannot change what you have not yet learned to see.

I have learned to read the world through a different lens, watching how it reacts to my daughter, how it welcomes her, and how it wounds her. Marcela is small in stature but vast in presence. At sixteen, she is a conference presenter, a public speaker, an international traveler, and a young woman who has survived fifteen surgeries with more grace than most adults muster in a lifetime. She carries the daily weight of the ableist gaze—stares, questions, assumptions—but she remains radiant, grounded, and joyfully herself.

One Saturday, we walked into our neighborhood store expecting nothing more than to buy ingredients for a family barbecue. The deli line was buzzing in its usual weekend way—children pointing at cookies, adults debating sandwiches, the soft hum of normal life. Then an employee leaned over the counter, looked down at my daughter, and brazenly asked in a loud voice: "Hey, how tall are you?" The question cut through the noise like a knife through warm butter. It wasn't curiosity—it was exposure. I felt Marcela shrink beside me, not because of her size, but because the world had once again attempted to make her a spectacle.

He quickly added, "I don't mean it in a bad way!" I wanted to snap back. I wanted to protect her with my teeth bared if I had to. But Marcela was watching me. I knew I had to model a better response than to bite his head off.

I don't know how I held it together enough to muster up the strength to calmly but unmistakably tell him his comment was rude and unacceptable. He kept trying to argue for his limitations, and I kept uttering the word *unacceptable* as I fought the tears back. I think he saw that my heart was broken. He disappeared into the back, and the deli fell silent. Everyone had heard. Everyone had seen. Deafening silence drifted through the air.

Marcela whispered, "Mom, please don't make a big deal." But mothers know when silence is betrayal.

The manager came out and apologized. I stood there, spoke truth to power as tears gently slid down my cheek. The profound damage lingered. For days, I could not erase that moment. Marcela tossed and turned with it too. I could let it go, shrink in silence, and pretend it did not happen; but hate and anger were not okay either.

I went back the next day—because justice, in our family, is a form of love. I told the store manager what had happened and why it mattered, why words matter, why presence matters, why the smallest comments can do the deepest harm.

But it was Marcela's voice that transformed that conversation, that moment, that experience. When she opened her mouth, it was as if beautiful poetry flowed out. I don't remember her exact words. I just remember how they made me feel. She explained, with heartbreaking clarity, how the experience made her feel—embarrassed, exposed, and reduced. It caught her off guard; she wasn't prepared in that moment, in that space, for the need to be armed. And then she said: "I don't want to get him in trouble or to get him fired. I just want him to understand. I want him to know his words matter. I want him to know that he hurt me, and he made me feel like there was something wrong with who I am."

Me? I wasn't quite as generous. My instinct was to shield, to correct, to fight back against a system that keeps wounding her. But she—my daughter—chose grace as her strategy and truth as her offering.

We asked for the chance to share her story with the staff, to widen their understanding of disability, belonging, and impact. We are still waiting.

But that is why this story belongs in this book. Because this is what ableism looks like *today*—quiet, casual, hiding in plain sight. And because this is what resistance looks like: a young disabled girl choosing to teach the world how to be better than the world has been to her.

Someone once told us that truth cannot be silenced. So here is hers, offered not from the wound, but from the wisdom born out of it.

ꕥ

As the universe would have it, because the universe has a way of balancing wounds with invitations, two weeks after the Honor Society debacle, Marcela and I were invited to present our talk The Power of the Heart at the national Skeletal Dysplasia Conference.

I remember thinking, almost bitterly at first, *how ironic.* One moment my daughter is cropped out of a photograph, invisible at an event meant to celebrate her. And the next, she is being positioned at the center of a conversation about love, humanity, and justice.

But life teaches in spirals, not lines. What we do not heal the first time returns, offering us another chance to learn.

And she did more than shine—she radiated. This time, she wasn't placed behind anyone. She wasn't spoken for. She wasn't accommodated—she was amplified. When she began speaking, there was no hesitancy, no self-consciousness, no shrinking. Just Marcela being fully, brilliantly herself: sharp-witted, courageous, truthful, funny, and deeply loving.

Families sat up instantly, curious about what she would say. Teens her age soaked up her stories. Siblings of kids with disabilities began asking her questions they had rarely dared ask anyone. Adults wept quietly as the conversation evolved, not from pity, but from recognition.

What should have been a concise presentation lasted more than an hour and thirty minutes. Families lingered to speak with us afterwards. Marcela was invited to consider doing this work from the platform of a beauty pageant, and we were invited to join a podcast. These connections were formed because no one wanted it to end. Everyone in that room craved more. More love, more connection, more change.

There was laughter, loud, free laughter that shook the room at moments. There were tears, of release, of resonance, of finally being understood. There was connection, the kind that bypasses intellect and lands directly in the chest. And there was healing, the unmistakable kind that only happens when truth is spoken in community.

In that room, I watched Marcela become something she had been all along: a leader, a teacher, a mirror, a catalyst.

Here she was, this child who had been pushed to the back of a group photo, commanding a room full of educators, parents, and professionals with nothing more than her honesty and her heart.

That night, as people thanked her, Marcela smiled—the smile of someone who knows she is seen. In that moment, she taught me again what I keep learning from her: We cannot control whether the world wounds us, but we can choose to love our way to the other side of adversity.

That conference became her platform to advocate and to say that we can learn from our mistakes, we can do better, we can turn invisibility into illumination. Marcela turned what hurt her into something holy.

9

Learning Forward

I HAVE LEARNED THAT WHEN a community harms your child, whether intentionally or not, you feel the rupture in your bones. But when another community sees your child fully, you feel the repair just as deeply. The tension between those two moments left something alive inside me, an urgency, a clarity, a steady insistence: We cannot stay where harm found us. We must move toward where love wants to lead us.

After the Honor Society ordeal, I carried a quiet heaviness as I realized that good, educated, well-intentioned adults still lacked the tools to create true belonging. They did not have the courage to love in action.

I understood then that knowing better is not the same as *being* better. And being better is not the same as *building* better. So I did what I have always done: I turned to the work, a search for how to transform harm into understanding, how to turn exclusion into pedagogy, and how to let love lead me toward a more just world.

ꕥ

As an educator, I cannot experience injustice without also asking myself *What does this teach us? What does this reveal about our systems? How will we do differently because of it?*

I began thinking in frameworks, because that is how my mind works, and suddenly the Honor Society night became more than a personal story. It became a case study in the social construction of disability, the pedagogy of belonging, and the mechanics of exclusion.

Every gesture, every oversight, every "small thing"—from the inaccessible stage, to the seating arrangement, to asking students to stand, to placing Marcela behind the group—was a lesson in how ableism is not always cruel; sometimes it is simply unexamined.

But unexamined harm is harm nonetheless. So I asked myself *What do we do with unexamined harm? How do we teach a community to see what it has never been taught to notice? How do we expand the moral imagination?*

This is where love became more than an emotion or ideal. It became praxis. The kind of love Freire names: critical, dialogical, liberatory. The kind of love bell hooks names: ethical, courageous, world-making. The kind of love The Power of the Heart explores: relational, conscious, embodied.

Love as praxis is not soft. It is rigorous, structural—a discipline. And in that discipline, I understood that even harm, especially harm, could be turned into curriculum, into dialogue, into reform, into a call to action.

It dawned on me that Marcela was teaching more than any of us realized. She had taught me courage. She had taught her siblings empathy. She had taught conference attendees truth-telling. And she had given educators a chance to become better. I began to see her not as the child harmed but as the child who illuminated the pathway forward. Her story was not a setback, it was a syllabus—if we let it be.

Some people look at Marcela and see what she cannot do. But I have spent my life witnessing what she *creates*, simply by being: connection, curiosity, disruption, reimagining, tenderness, humor, and grace, leading to a different vision of a life worth living.

Marcela moves through the world as though it were built for her, because in my heart, it always was. That is the human spirit, too: the refusal to shrink to fit the world, and the invitation for the world to expand instead.

ᔓ

After that conference, I felt something inside me shift and settle into place. The question was no longer *Why did this happen?* The question now was *What will we do now?* And the answer came back, steady and clear: We learn forward. We lead with love. We redesign belonging. Because, as Marcela has shown us, we can grow if we choose to.

I now understand that the work of belonging is not about avoiding harm: It is about repairing it, together, through love that listens, acts, and leads.

10

What We Learn From the Edges

I HAVE COME TO UNDERSTAND that the world reveals itself most honestly at the edges.

Edges are the places where systems fray just enough to expose their inner workings, where the stories we tell about inclusion and belonging fall apart under the weight of lived experience. Growing up, I believed that the center was where safety lived, where legitimacy was affirmed. But mothering Marcela taught me something radically different: *The edges are where truth lives.*

Through Marcela's life, I have been escorted to the borderlands of identity, disability, education, and belonging—not as an academic observer, but as a participant. These spaces have become my classrooms—the sites where I study power, tenderness, exclusion, and the possibilities that awkwardly but insistently push their way toward liberation.

bell hooks wrote that love is "an act of will—both an intention and an action." What she did not say, but what

I have lived, is that love also makes us students. Love forces us to learn what we did not ask to learn by taking us to the edges, places where comfort is replaced by clarity. It asks us to look directly at the things we once had the privilege not to see.

And the edges are never abstract. They show up in small moments: Marcela's wheelchair stuck between two rows of desks not designed for her body; a curriculum that labels her as "student with needs" but rarely labels the system's limitations; a school photo where she is cropped out, and the silence that followed. These are not merely inconveniences or oversights. They are data points, ethnographies of exclusion. They reveal the gap between intention and impact. They tell the truth about the structures we live within, structures that behave exactly as they were designed to behave.

But the edges also show something else: resistance. Marcela's resistance is rarely loud, but it is always steady. It is present in the way she names what is unfair—not to cast blame, but to invite honesty. It is in the way she speaks her truth with a clarity that adults often mistake for boldness, when in fact it is simply her refusal to pretend. It is in the way she smiles at herself in the mirror before a presentation, reminding me that confidence is a muscle grown through being seen.

And it is in the way she expands a room.

When we presented The Power of the Heart just weeks after the Honor Society incident, something remarkable happened. Marcela's voice, her humor, her fierceness, her refusal to shrink, pulled people toward her.

Her presence shifts dynamics. Her story reminds us that belonging is not a favor others grant—it is a human right we each carry, whether the world makes room for it or not.

As a scholar, I have engaged the theories that help us name these dynamics: Disability as a socially constructed margin. Identity as an ongoing negotiation. Belonging as a layered practice.

Yet as a mother I know these concepts in my body. I know them through every moment where I have had to hold my breath, make a decision, or speak truth to power. My research sharpened my language. Marcela sharpened my courage. When I combine the two, my scholarship and my motherhood, what emerges is a new kind of clarity: Living at the edges has not weakened us. It has refined us. Marcela and I have learned to read between the lines of systems designed without us in mind. We have learned to trust the wisdom that lives in our own stories. We have learned that the edge is not a place of exile—it is a vantage point, one from which we can see everything. And perhaps this is the real curriculum of belonging: learning to live so intentionally that the edges become not places of harm, but places where new worlds begin.

11

Unapologetically Relearning

THERE IS A MOMENT IN every journey when the world you thought you understood becomes too small for the truth you now carry. After the conference, after Marcela's radiance filled that room, I felt something shifting inside me—a recalibration of what I believed about change, about community, about the work of rewriting identity.

I realized I had spent years teaching, writing, and lecturing about inclusive practices, identity development, and the politics of belonging. But suddenly, none of that felt like enough. Because the real work wasn't happening in classrooms or conference rooms: It was happening in the quiet spaces where harm and hope collide. It was happening in the lived curriculum of my daughter's life.

After the Honor Society incident, we continued reflecting on what people at the school "should have" done differently, as if inclusion were a checklist, as if belonging were a procedural compliance issue, as if the absence of an accessible ramp could be solved by a single policy revision. But the truth I felt settling into me was this: Belonging requires a transformation of vision, not a modification of logistics. People have to relearn how to see. They have to see the child in the wheelchair not as an exception, but as part of the whole. They have to see the ramp not as an accommodation, but as an invitation. They have to see difference not as a burden, but as a teacher. But sight like that does not come naturally in an ableist world. It is learned, unlearned, and learned again.

Sitting in my office after the conference, surrounded by schoolwork and research articles, I felt a strange mix of grief and clarity. The grief was present because I realized how many in my own academic environment, in a field that prides itself on progressive values, still failed to see my daughter. The clarity arose because I knew, finally, that my work could no longer remain in the realm of theory.

Marcela had become my teacher in ways that no journal article ever could, through her ability to move through exclusion without surrendering her joy, her instinct to respond to harm with humor instead of bitterness. She taught me relational wisdom. It wasn't about overcoming disability; it was about transforming the space around her.

It hit me then that identity development isn't an individual project: It's communal. Watching Marcela at the conference, surrounded by children, adults, siblings, and educators who suddenly saw her not as a problem to solve but a person to learn from, I understood that identity is shaped not just by what is reflected back to us but by what we refuse to absorb.

Marcela refuses to absorb shame, limits, the narratives that society hands her. She sees herself clearly, even when others don't. And that terrifies and inspires people in equal measure.

That night, after the conference, she climbed into the car exhausted but glowing. She asked if I thought she had done well. I told her the truth: "You didn't just do well, Marcela. You shifted something in everyone."

She nodded and leaned back, looking out the window as the city lights blurred into ribbons. "I think they needed to see me," she said—not with arrogance, but with knowing.

I realized then that this work—this book—was not about documenting events or critiquing systems. It was about vision. About learning to see differently. About teaching others to see with their hearts instead of their habits.

12

Love Letters to My Daughter

Public Love as Restoration

THERE ARE MOMENTS IN a mother's life when love must travel beyond the walls of the home. Moments when love must stand in the street, take a microphone, open its chest, and say: "You will not diminish my child. You will not define her. I will love her louder than you can wound her."

For years, I wrote to Marcela in the most public way I knew—social media posts that were less *announcements* and more *rituals*. I did not know why I was doing it, but I knew that it felt right to do it. They were messages where I could reaffirm her worth in a world that so often tried to negotiate it. These letters became a written archive of our love, our fight, and our becoming.

What follows are some of those love letters—unfiltered, bilingual, imperfect, and true.

ꟹ

Letter 1: A Beginning—Spanish [original]

Un día una niña despertó temprano por la mañana llena de alegría y entusiasmada por la idea de que iba de excursión. Pues, ese día, la niña y su familia iban al zoológico para compensar unos días duros que habían pasado.

Ella era feliz y libre para disfrutar del esplendor de la naturaleza, pero a medida que la familia recorría los caminos en el parque, la niña se volvió triste y dolorida. Al preguntarle que le pasaba, respondió: "¡mira, como todos me miran!"

Ella era digna de ver; recientemente operada, pero llena de vida, fuerte y aprovechando su oportunidad de volver a ser niña y pasarlo bien.

Pero la niña, tan digna de ver, atraía las miradas de todos los niños y padres que se encontraban por el camino y las miradas le hacían sentirse mal. Tan mal que con el corazón pesado, ella exclamó: "ojala que la gente no me mirara, y simplemente dijera hola."

En ese momento, desde el corazón de esa niña, nació un mensaje "Solo di hola" (Just Say Hi) enfocado a todos aquellos niños y padres que no pueden contener sus miradas. Es un mensaje de amor que destaca que todos somos iguales y si paráramos a conocer al uno al otro, podríamos descubrirlo.

"Just Say Hi" es el mensaje de Marcela Rey Serghini y esta camiseta representa un acto de solidaridad en apoyo a Marcela y su familia en su misión de concienciar a las personas de la importancia de respetar las diferencias y ser amable.

¡Llévala con amor!

English Translation

One day, a little girl woke up early in the morning full of happiness and excited by the idea that she was going on

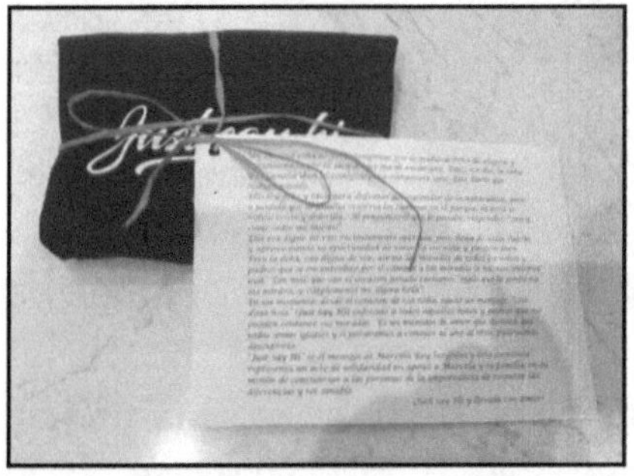

Each "Just Say Hi" shirt was wrapped with a carefully tied red ribbon and accompanied by a letter relating the origin of the message so that everyone who wore it would carry not just fabric but also meaning.

a trip. Well, that day, the little girl and her family were going to the zoo to make up for the new hard days that they had gone through.

She was happy and free to enjoy the splendor of nature, but as the family walked through the paths of the park, the little girl became sad and hurt. When she was asked what was wrong, she responded, "Look how everyone looks at me."

She was worthy of looking at, recently operated on, but full of life, strong and taking advantage of her change, her return to being a kid and having a good time.

But the girl, so worthy of being seen, attracted the gaze of all the kids and parents who she encountered along her path, and their gazes made her feel bad. So bad, that with a heavy heart, she exclaimed, "I wish people would not stare at me, and would simply say hello."

In that moment, from the heart of that little girl, a message was born: "Solo di hola" (Just Say Hi) focusing on all the kids and parents who could not contain their gaze. It is a message of love that highlights that we are all the same, and if we stop to learn about one another, we can discover it.

"Just Say Hi" is Marcela Rey Serghini's message, and this shirt represents an act of solidarity to support Marcela and her family in their mission to raise awareness about the importance of respective differences and being kind.

Wear it with love!

∽

Letter 2: A Birthday Wish (Age 12)—Spanish [original]

Amo a todos mis niños por igual, cada uno es un regalo que me ha traído, junto con una felicidad profunda, un gran sentido de pertenecía que me une a este mundo y marca un rumbo claro que perseguir. Pero, el día de hoy, lo vivo de forma diferente. Todos los 5 de febrero, desde hace 12 años ya, despierto con emociones incógnitas. Con otros sentimientos internos que sacuden mi mundo y que me hacen recordar la gran suerte que me ha caído encima.

Cada 5 de febrero revivo como no han sabido apostar por ti y me asombro cómo demuestras tu gran presencia. Cada 5 de febrero me sirve como ejemplo de cómo triunfar a base de fuerzas interiores y visiones de otras posibilidades. Cada 5 de febrero soy más consciente de que el tiempo vuela y que no se puede desperdiciar ningún momento ni ninguna oportunidad.

Hoy, con el mundo al revés, el día de tu cumpleaños significa aún más para mi. Demuestra que con pequeños pasos podemos fundar otro camino. Ilumina que el obstáculo es, en realidad, una oportunidad de crear algo nuevo y comprobar que nada es imposible. Y simboliza que unidos somos más; más empáticos, más justos, más imaginativos.

Sí, sí, cada 5 de febrero es un gran día para mi. Un día que vivo con mucha ilusión y llena de la esperanza que los siguientes 364 días sean iguales de profundos que los anteriores.

Marcela, te deseo que seas feliz, feliz en tu día . . . y quiero que sepas que haces que el mundo sea mejor.

Happy 12th Birthday, I love you so much!

English Translation

I love all my children equally; each one is a gift that has brought me profound happiness and a deep sense of belonging that anchors me to this world and gives me a clear path to follow. But today, I live it differently. Every February 5th, for the past 12 years, I have wakened with unfamiliar

Marcela on her 12th birthday, wearing a fresh flower crown and feeling proud to be seen.

emotions—internal stirrings that shake my world and remind me of the incredible luck that has fallen upon me.

Every February 5th, I relive how some people failed to believe in you, and I marvel at how you reveal your powerful presence. Every February 5th teaches me once again how to triumph through inner strength and visions of alternative possibilities. Every February 5th makes me more aware of how fast time flies and how no moment or opportunity should be wasted.

Today, with the world upside down, your birthday means even more to me. It shows that with small steps we can create another path. It illuminates that obstacles are truly opportunities to create something new and to confirm that nothing is impossible. And it symbolizes that together we are more—more empathetic, more just, more imaginative.

Yes, yes, every February 5th is a great day for me. A day I live with hope and the wish that the next 364 days are as profound as the ones that just came before it.

Marcela, I wish you happiness—true happiness—on your day…and I want you to know that you make the world better.

Happy 12th Birthday. I love you so much!

ഗ

Letter 3: A Birthday Wish (Age 13)—Spanish [original]

Hoy es 5 de febrero y como es costumbre, me estallo con las ganas que tengo de gritar "FELICIDADES MARCELA, ERES INCREIBLE" ¡OMG, hoy cumples 13 años! Sabias que el número 13 tiene varios significados interesantes. Entre otros, simboliza la desaparición de lo material, el nacimiento del espíritu, y el paso a un nivel superior de la existencia. Abrazo este año con muchísima ilusión para averiguar las magníficas oportunidades que te va a traer. Yo puedo corroborar que este año ya se va notando un poco diferente (aún todavía estás durmiendo a la hora que es, como una autentica adolescente, jiji).

Pero, en serio, me doy cuenta de que te alejas de mi poco a poco. Me encanta ver como has empezado a buscar tus propias repuestas y a confiar en otros para sus consejos y sabiduría. Aunque me entristezca perder "el bebe" en ti, no me deprimo del todo, porque sé que es lo mejor que puedes hacer. Ole tú, por desarrollar tus propios recursos y buscar otras fuentes de información, lo vas a necesitar para poder navegar mejor por este mundo tan tumultuoso.

También veo, cada vez con más claridad, que has prendido tu propio camino. Ya, tus sueños son cada vez más tuyos, de una persona mayor y de una persona más independiente. No buscas tanto la conformación, y no necesitas tanto la aprobación de mamá, aunque de vez en cuando te gusta comprobar que la tienes.

Cada día te veo más—más fuerte, más ambiciosa, más llena de vida, más mujer—y cada día más capaz de hacer grandes cosas en el mundo. Me encanta que eres fiel a los tuyos, honesta en momentos difíciles, trabajadora hasta el último momento. Admiro como te levantas cada día y agarras por los cuernos a la vida e insistes en que tú puedes más. Tomo nota de ti y crezco a tu lado.

Simplemente, estoy profundamente agradecida, por tenerte en mi vida y por tener la oportunidad de aprender de un alma tan sabia como la tuya.

Happy Birthday my sweet baby girl. You make me so happy!

Marcela on her thirteenth birthday, where joy was effortless and the spirit bright.

English Translation
Today is February 5th, and as usual, I'm bursting with the urge to shout, "CONGRATULATIONS MARCELA, YOU ARE AMAZING!" OMG, today you turn 13! Did you know that the number 13 has several interesting meanings? Among others, it symbolizes the disappearance of the material, the birth of the spirit, and the passage to a higher level of existence. I embrace this year with so much excitement, eager to discover the magnificent opportunities it will bring you. I can already confirm that this year feels a little different (you're still sleeping at this hour, like a true teenager, hehe).

But seriously, I'm noticing how you're slowly moving away from me. I love seeing how you've begun to search for your own answers and rely on others for their advice and wisdom. Even though it saddens me to lose "the baby" in you, I'm not truly depressed, because I know it's the best thing you can do. Good for you, for developing your own resources and looking for other sources of information—you'll need that to navigate this tumultuous world.

I also see, with growing clarity, that you've lit your own path. Your dreams now belong more to you—dreams of someone older, more independent. You don't seek conformity as much, and you don't need my approval the way you used to, although every now and then you like to check that you still have it.

Every day I see more of you—stronger, more ambitious, more full of life, more woman—and each day more capable of doing great things in the world. I love that you are loyal to your people, honest in difficult moments, and hardworking until the last minute. I admire how you rise each day and grab life by the horns, insisting that you can do more. I take note of you and grow at your side.

I am simply, profoundly grateful to have you in my life and to have the chance to learn from a soul as wise as yours.

Happy Birthday, my sweet baby girl. You make me so happy!

Letter 4: Dulce, 16 Marcela—Spanish [original]

Hoy es tu decimosexto cumpleaños. Como dicta la tradición, no podía dejar que el día pasara sin gritarle al mundo lo increíblemente asombrada que estoy por la persona en la que te estás convirtiendo. Dieciséis es un número muy importante, ¿sabes? Por fin puedes obtener tu licencia de conducir y empezar a "adultizar" de una nueva manera—aunque no te recomiendo apresurarte con eso, eh.

Sé cuánto te encanta la matemática; ¿sabías que 16 es un cuadrado perfecto de 4? No hay muchos números así. Y como me encanta lo espiritual que eres, déjame añadir esto: el número 16 simboliza renacimiento y nuevos comienzos.

Y como sabes cuánto amo las mariposas, ¿sabías que las orugas tienen 16 patitas? Y esas pequeñas criaturas se transforman en las mariposas que tanto adoro. Dieciséis es, sin duda, un número importante.

Durante dieciséis años has sido una luz brillante en mi camino, empujándome a crecer y evolucionar hacia mejores maneras de estar en el mundo. Durante dieciséis años has llenado mi copa, y mi corazón rebosa de amor. Durante dieciséis años has modelado cómo ser la mejor versión de uno mismo, y has demostrado lo que significa ser determinada, reflexiva y amorosa.

Recuerdo el día en que te conocí hace dieciséis años. Estaba allí entonces, maravillada por tu perfección, tal como estoy ahora, de la misma manera, aún asombrada por ti.

No hay palabras que describan cuánto te amo, mi dulce niña. A medida que empiezas a abrir tus alas y volar como las majestuosas mariposas que tanto me gustan, recuerda siempre que el mundo es un lugar mejor contigo en él. Ten presente que la manera en que te presentas importa, y que tienes una contribución que hacer que es únicamente tuya.

Verás y escucharás cosas que ojalá no tuvieras que ver ni escuchar. Para esos momentos, recuerda que eres amada, y que tu valor no está definido por el mundo exterior, sino por quién eres por dentro. Sé siempre tú misma, y haz que cuente.

El más feliz de los cumpleaños para ti, mi hermosa niña.

Love always,
—mommy

English Translation

Sweet, sweet Marcela. Today is your sweet 16th birthday. As per tradition, I could not let the day pass without shouting to the world how incredibly amazed I am by who you are becoming. Sixteen is a very important number you know. You can finally get your driver's license and start adulting in a new way, although I do not recommend you rush to do that, eh.

I know how you love math; did you realize that 16 is a perfect square of 4? There are not too many of those. And because I love how spiritual you are, let me add that the number 16 signifies rebirth and new beginnings. Also, you know

At sixteen, Marcela's light was not accidental; it was earned. Her courage matured into resolve and her joy into intention. I am so grateful to walk by her side and watch her rise.

I love butterflies, did you know that caterpillars have 16 legs, and they turn into those butterflies? Sixteen is an important number indeed.

For sixteen years you have been a light shining bright on my path, pushing me to grow and evolve into better ways of being. For sixteen years, you have filled my cup, and my heart overflows with love. For sixteen years you have modeled how to be the best version of one's self, and demonstrated what it means to be driven yet thoughtful and loving.

I remember the day I met you sixteen years ago. I stood there then, in awe of your perfection, just as I stand here now in that same way, amazed by you.

No words describe how much I love you, my sweet girl. As you start to spread your wings and fly like the majestic butterflies I love so much, always remember that the world is a better place with you in it. Know that how you show up matters and that you have a contribution to make that is uniquely yours. You will see and hear things that I wish you did not have to. For those moments, know that you are loved and that your worth is defined not by the external world but by who you are within. Always be you and make it count! Happiest of birthdays to you, my beautiful baby girl.

Love always,

—Mommy

❧

Letter 5: Thoughts on Discrimination, Empathy, and Courage—Spanish [original]

¡No estás sola! Compartimos contigo ésta lucha. Nosotros también deseamos que nuestro mundo sea más justo, más comprensivo y más empático. De hecho, creemos que es trabajo de todos y hay muchas personas que fallan. ¿"Por qué todo el mundo me mira?" nos preguntas. Quizás por curiosidad, desconocimiento, o por su propio ego... a saber.

Que sepas, que estamos orgullosos de ti, de tu manera de enfrentar la injusticia y la discriminación. Admiramos tu esfuerzo y tus ganas de sentir paz. Ayer nos preguntaste: "¿si yo no tuviera mi discapacidad, estaríamos igual de preocupados por la discriminación?" Lamentamos decirte que lo más probable es que no, estamos aprendiendo todo esto contigo y ahora sabemos que es uno de los valiosos regalos que has aportado a nuestra vida. Nos has enseñado a vivir con una profunda empatía hacia los demás, y es nuestra obligación poner nuestro grano de arena en la lucha contra el sufrimiento de las personas discriminadas.

Te cuento un secreto, cuando eras un bebe, ya sabíamos que esto iba a ser difícil, que el mundo no estaba preparado para ti, pero es ahora cuando estás descubriendo esa realidad. Que ahora te vas dando cuenta de en qué tipo de sociedad vivimos. Que estamos en una sociedad poco humana, no protegemos a nuestros vulnerables y tenemos una tendencia hacia un estereotipo de normalidad en la que no todos encajamos.

Siento decirte que siempre vas a tener que luchar, pero que sepas, que por mucho que sufras con cada mirada, chismeo u obstáculo que encuentras en el camino, te vamos a querer y apoyar aún más. Te estamos educando no solo para que conozcas tus derechos sino también para exigirlos y amarte a ti misma. Tienes un trabajo importante en esta sociedad y también tienes tu lugar, pero como dice un sabio poeta "caminante no hay camino, se hace camino al andar." Por mucho que quieras ser como los demás, va a ser difícil porque tú has nacido para brillar.

Ahora, levántate y da otro paso. Nunca dejes de querer un mundo con amor, más justo y con más empatía, es lo que necesitamos todos.

¡Te queremos Marcela!

—Mamá y Papá

English Translation

You are not alone! We share in this struggle with you. We, too, want our world to be more just, more understanding, and more empathetic. In fact, we believe it's everyone's responsibility, and many people fail at it. "Why is everyone looking at me?" you ask. Perhaps out of curiosity, ignorance, or their own ego . . . who knows.

Know that we are proud of you—of the way you face injustice and discrimination. We admire your effort and your longing for peace. Yesterday you asked us, "If I didn't have my disability, would we be as concerned about discrimination?" We're sorry to say that probably not. We are learning all of this with you, and now we understand that this is one of the precious gifts you've brought into our lives. You've taught us to live with profound empathy toward others, and it's our responsibility to contribute to the fight against the suffering of discriminated people.

Let me tell you a secret: When you were a baby, we already knew this would be difficult—that the world wasn't prepared for you. But only now are you discovering that reality. Now you are noticing what kind of society we live in.

Marcela became the face of a social justice campaign with a message both simple and profound: disability is human. She was more than a diagnosis; and her condition, spondyloepiphyseal dysplasia, was only part of her journey. Disability neither defined her nor determined where she could go.

Right before the start of a new school year, Marcela and other volunteers from the Just Say Hi campaign handed out wooden pencils, each one carrying a quiet reminder that one's potential is already there, just like the graphite inside the pencil. It simply needs sharpening through education and understanding. Attached to each pencil was a card that read: "A new school year means new opportunities. Just Say Hi. Be a good person. Be kind. Be different."

A defining milestone: Marcela's first presentation at the University of Cádiz. What began as a grassroots social justice campaign evolved into a platform for her to speak truth to power and to share her experiences. She embodied the bridge between lived experience and institutional dialogue as she shared how her advocacy work not only raised awareness, but liberated her, giving her voice, strength, and purpose. Advocacy for her isn't just policy and politics; it is something far more accessible and far more transformative: kindness.

Marcela was doing more than inviting the community to an event; she was carrying forward a movement that had already taken her into the streets. Behind her rested a powerful symbol of that journey: the poster she held during the disability awareness march in Cádiz earlier that day. Its quote from The Little Prince *by Antoine de Saint-Exupéry, "what is essential is invisible to the eye," was more than literary; it was a guiding philosophy. It became the perfect backdrop for her call to action: the inaugural citywide Festival de Inclusión. This festival, a bold collaboration among local Spanish associations, went beyond raising awareness. Marcela's vision was celebration. People were invited to celebrate difference and each other. Soccer players signed autographs for children. Flamenco dancers, singers, and guitarists filled the streets with the soul of Spanish folklore. Color, texture, and creativity infused every corner. That day difference was honored.*

We live in a society lacking humanity; we don't protect our vulnerable; and we cling to a stereotype of normality into which not all of us fit.

I'm sorry to tell you that you will always have to fight, but know that every time you suffer—because of a stare, a whisper, or an obstacle on the path—we will love and support you even more. We are raising you not only to know your rights but to demand them and to love yourself. You have important work to do in this society, and you also have your place. But as a wise poet says, "Traveler, there is no path; the path is made by walking." As much as you may want to be like everyone else, it will be difficult, because you were born to shine.

Now, get up and take another step. Never stop wanting a world full of love, justice, and empathy—because that is what we all need.

We love you, Marcela.
—Mommy and Dad

Letter 6: Thoughts on Middle School and Letting Go—Spanish [original]

La semana pasada fueron mis hijos menores quienes empezaron en el colegio. Esta semana es mi hija mayor, y que no solo comienza un nuevo curso escolar, pero pasa a una etapa en su vida que ya marcará de forma definitiva su futuro—al instituto.

No hay palabras para describir la emoción que siento. Es un poco de miedo mezclado con un pellizco de tristeza y un toque de felicidad.

De forma egoísta, he pensado, "ojalá que pudiera hacerlo yo por ella" para evitar los baches y los chichones, pero luego, verle crecer, luchar por alcanzar sus objetivos, y abrir caminos hacia un mejor futuro, me llena de tanto orgullo y admiración y me doy cuenta que la tengo que soltar.

Avanza, hija mía, en esta nueva etapa con plena confianza en ti misma, de saber que estás justo donde tienes que estar, no porque te lo han regalado, sino porque eres una guerrera que has reclamado tu sitio. Aprovecha todas las batallas que te vas a encontrar en el camino para redefinir el orden establecido y crear nuevas posibilidades. Cree en tu fuerza interior, porque te ha servido a ti, a mí y a muchas otras personas cómo ejemplo para plantear mejor las cuestiones de la justica. Aprende todo lo que puedas, porque esto es una oportunidad única y hay que exprimirla, especialmente si quieres llegar a ser, como tú dices una "dentista, secretario del estado o presidente."

No olvides nunca, mi amor, que el tamaño no importa cuando la mente esté bien adiestrada y el corazón repleto de amor.

Rise . . . and go out there and shine.
You amaze me!

English Translation

Last week my youngest children started school. This week it is my oldest child, who not only begins a new school year, but embarks on a new stage in her life that will greatly influence the outcome of her future—middle school.

There are no words to describe the emotions that I feel. It's a bit like fear, mixed with a pinch of sadness, and a dash of happiness.

I wrote to Marcela on the first day of middle school because it felt so big. Middle school was not just a new chapter; it was another place where she would learn to belong. Her smile was bright with becoming, her spirit already leaning forward. This moment was not bigger than the resolve she already carried within her.

Sometimes I think, "I wish I could do it for her" so that she avoids the bumps and bruises. However, to watch her grow, struggle to achieve her goals, and trailblaze toward a better future, floods me with pride and admiration and I know that I must let her go.

Move forward, my child, in this stage of your life with full confidence in yourself, knowing that you are where you were meant to be, not because someone placed you there, but because you are a warrior that can claim her victory. Take advantage of all the battles you will encounter along the way to redefine the established order and create new possibilities. Believe in your inner strength, because it has served you, me, and many others as an example of how better to engage with questions of justice. Learn all that you can, for this is a unique opportunity to be maximized, especially if you are to become, as you say, "a dentist, madam secretary or president."

Never forget, my love, that size does not matter when the mind is disciplined and the heart full of love.

Rise . . . and go out there and shine.

You amaze me!

ʚɞ

Letter 7: Resilience & Faith—Spanish [original]

Round 1 — prueba superada. Ganadora declarada. You win. Round 2 begins now . . .

De pequeña, he imaginado la vida como algo linear. Y que el propósito era moverse del punto A al punto B para tener la recompensa. Pero a medida que he ido madurando, he visto que la vida es dinámica, y que está repleta de curvas, altibajos,

Some days are for leaning in, and some days are for fighting back. This photo captures a sacred pause, faith over fear, finding comfort and quiet strength in each other's arms before surgery. In that moment, courage looked like closeness.

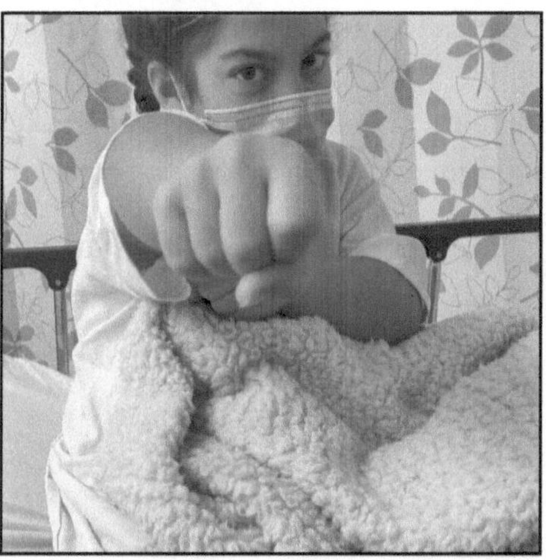

Here stands our warrior. Fist raised, masked up, heart unwavering. A reminder that no matter how big the obstacle, the spirit within us remains unbroken. Marcela has never waited for what comes next, she meets it.

y cambios de sentido radicales. Lo único seguro que tenemos es la inseguridad, porque no hay forma de saber con certeza a dónde vamos, hay que seguir aprendiendo a dar el siguiente mejor paso.

Las circunstancias se han presentado y los astros se han alineado para traernos a este lugar desconocido. Y aunque el viento sopla fuerte, y apenas tengo los pies en el suelo, y el rumbo que marca la veleta es impreciso, tengo fe. Fe en que el universo sabe más que yo y que el destino se aproxima... siento las posibilidades.

Te tengo, te agarro, no te soltaré nunca por muy fuerte que sea nuestra tormenta o muy turbio que sea el camino a nuestro destino. Contigo siempre he tenido la suerte de ver con claridad. Has venido a este mundo cuándo has querido, cómo has querido, dejando tu huella dónde has pasado. Contigo he aprendido que ni un minuto antes, ni un minuto después, solo en el momento preciso. Así que, te tengo, te agarro y no te suelto hasta el momento justo. Tengo fe en ti y en tu fuerza.

Eternally grateful to learn from you. If anyone can do this, it's you.

All my love always,
—Mommy

English Translation

Round 1 — Test passed. Winner declared. You win.
Round 2 — starts now...

When I was younger, I used to think that life was linear and that the purpose of it was to move from point A to point B to obtain a reward.

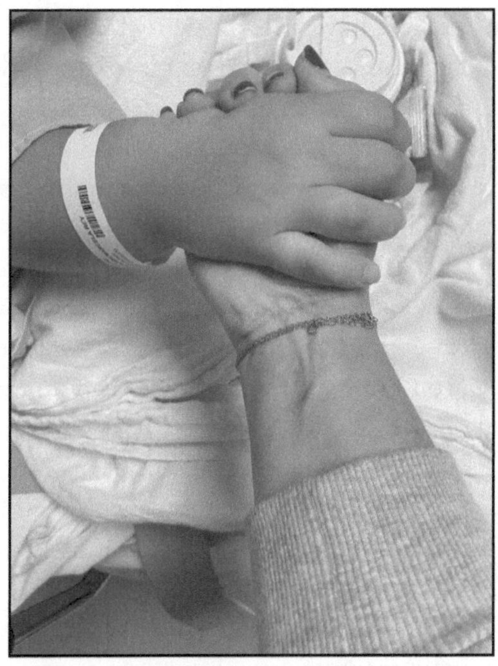

With love as our anchor, our hands are steady, and our hearts unyielding.

But, as I grew up, I began to notice just how dynamic life is, full of curves, ups and downs, and radical changes of direction. I learned that the only certain thing is that things are uncertain. There is no way to know with certainty where we are going, only that we must continue learning how to take the next best step.

Circumstances have been presented, and the stars have aligned to bring us to this unknown place. And although the wind blows fiercely, I barley have my feet on the ground, and the needle on the compass is wavering, I have faith. Faith that the universe knows more than I, and that destiny is close . . . I can feel the possibilities.

I have faith. I got you and I won't let go no matter how strong the storm is or how uncertain the path to our density becomes. With you, I have always been lucky enough to see with clarity. You came into this world when you wanted, as you wanted, leaving your footprint where you passed. With you, I have learned that neither one minute before nor one minute after, only at the precise moment. Therefore, I have you, I hold you and I won't let go until just the right time. I have faith in you and your strength.

So here I am, holding you with faith in you, in your strength, in your destiny.

Eternally grateful to learn from you. If anyone can do this, it's you.

All my love always,

—Mommy

ೲ

Letter 8: En el otro lado de la puerta—Spanish [original]
Marcela, estoy aquí, en el otro lado de la puerta. Es una puerta grande y colorida; supongo que lo han hecho así para darle un toque de alegría , pero sigue siendo una puerta fría y una puerta que nos separa. Estoy aquí esperándote, esperando que me llamen y me digan que haya salido todo bien.

Ya sé que eres experta con todo esto, siempre me has sorprendida tu buena disposición y tu certeza ante la incertidumbre, pero yo no me acostumbro de dejarte allí, en el otro lado de esa puerta.

Es un espacio extraordinario, equipado con todo que puedes imaginar, para cuidarte lo mejor posible, pero es un sitio que impone. Y tú allí, pues tú brillas como siempre y que remedio que intentar seguir tus pautas. Respiro hondo, sonrío y te suelto.

No llores, digo a mi misma, pero difícil es resistir la tentación. Tus manos siguen pareciéndome iguales de pequeñitas que el primer día que te cogí en brazos. Y tu mirada, pues, me llena de tanta felicidad que me movería cualquier montaña para llegar a ti, y tú, pues tú me transmites un amor que me calma hasta el alma. Difícil no llorar por ti.

Aquí te espero, pensando en cómo tu eres parte de mi, entrelazadas somos en el mismo destino.

Aprovecho el vinculo para mandarte toda mi fuerza, como una ola que te aprieta el cuerpo lo justo para sentirte segura o como un rayo de sol que calienta la piel hasta notar paz en tu interior.

Ay mi Marcelita, tu me afirmas porque es importante saborear cada minuto, priorizar y agarrarme a lo que realmente

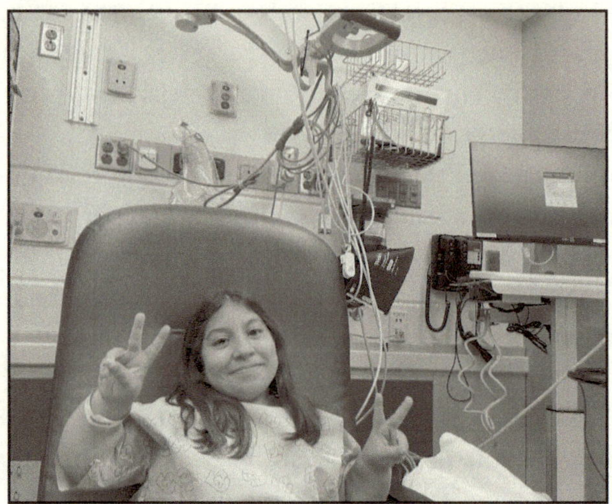

Marcela sitting in preop right before surgery surrounded by cables, monitors, and medical devices. She modeled a quiet kind of bravery that does not need to shout. It simply stands, smiles, and trusts. Even there, on the edge of uncertainty, she radiated peace, gently asking me to choose courage, light, and joy even when it would have been easier to choose fear.

vale, porque al final y al cabo solo tenemos una oportunidad de hacer la vida valer.

Aquí te espero, mi valiente Marcela, aquí estoy en el otro lado de la puerta, esperando para cogerte en brazos otra vez.

Get well soon, I love you so, so much!

English Translation

On the Other Side of the Door

Marcela, here I am on the other side of that door. It is a big and colorful door. I suppose that they made it that way to brighten this space up, but it is still a cold door and a door that separates us.

I am here, waiting. Waiting for them to call me, waiting for them to tell me that everything went well.

I know you are an expert at all of this. I have always been surprised by your positive disposition and your sense of certainty in the face of uncertainty, but I have never been able to get used to leaving you on the other side of that door.

It is an extraordinary space, equipped with everything you can imagine to provide you with the best possible care, but it is a place that imposes. And you, there, you shine like always, so what choice do I have but to follow your example. I breathe deep, smile, and let you go.

Don't cry, I tell myself. But it is hard to resist the temptation. Your hands still seem just as small as the first day I held you in my arms. The way you look at me fills me with so much joy that I would move any mountain just to get to you. And you, you transmit a love that reaches the depths of my soul, it is hard not to cry for you.

Here I am waiting for you, thinking about how our lives are entwined in the same destiny. I use this bond to send you all my strength, as a force that wraps around you and makes you feel safe or as the warmth of a sunbeam on your skin until you feel harmony on the inside.

Oh, my Marcela, you affirm for me why we must savor every moment, prioritize and hold on to the things that matter most because in the end we only have one chance to make this life count.

Here I wait, my brave Marcela, on the other side of that door, waiting to hold you in my arms again.

Get well soon. I love you so, so much.

13

Becoming Us

MOTHERHOOD HAS BEEN DESCRIBED in many ways—as sacrifice, devotion, responsibility—but for me, motherhood has been an act of transformation. Not a transformation that occurs in isolation but a relational one. The truth I have come to understand is simple and profound: We become through one another.

Becoming who we are is rarely a gentle unfolding. More often, it is a collision with truth.

I spent much of my early adulthood believing identity was something built: a set of achievements, roles, and expectations carefully stacked into shape. Daughter. Wife. Scholar. Mother. Advocate. Professional. I wore each one like a well-pressed garment, believing that becoming myself meant fitting them all flawlessly.

"Becoming us" is the framework through which I now understand my life, my motherhood, and my learning. It is the recognition that identity is shaped not solely by individual striving, but by the relationships that challenge us, reveal us, and invite us to grow.

Marcela is central to that becoming, not as an idea or symbol, but as a lived presence who has expanded my ways of knowing, listening, and being.

ꟹ

For many years, I believed the work of adulthood was self-definition: becoming who *I* was meant to be. But life, motherhood, illness, and lived experience taught me otherwise. The deepest growth did not emerge from isolation or personal ambition; it emerged from connection, especially the connections that demanded unlearning.

Marcela brought with her a new epistemology, one rooted in intuition, empathy, and the quiet truth that lives beneath language. Through her, I learned that meaning is co-created and that the heart teaches what the mind does not yet understand.

"Becoming us" is the name I give to that transformation.

Much of what I thought I knew—about ability, success, time, intelligence, identity—began to dissolve as I parented Marcela. She revealed a larger, deeper truth waiting underneath.

Marcela's presence invited me into that deeper truth. She taught me to listen with my heart instead of rushing to interpret. She taught me to hold silence as a space of meaning, not absence. The chapter of becoming her mother was also the chapter of becoming more human.

Throughout this book, I keep returning to a central truth: Lived experience is a teacher.

The more I reflect on this journey, the more I see that becoming a mother was never just about nurturing a child. It was about entering a relationship that reshaped my identity, my worldview, and my purpose.

Marcela made me braver, softer, more aware, more patient, more open. In learning to mother her, I learned to mother myself—gently, honestly, without judgment. This mutual transformation—her becoming, my becoming—is the essence of becoming us.

This book is about learning to see with new eyes, eyes shaped by lived experience, vulnerability, identity, disability, and love. "Becoming us" is the connective tissue that allows all these themes to speak to each other.

It is the explanation of how my heart expanded; how my identity was reshaped through motherhood and unlearning; and how Marcela's presence continues to transform my understanding of justice, belonging, and humanity.

"Becoming us" is not an event. It is an ongoing relational evolution. It is the story of two souls and lives intertwining, each one shaping the other. And it is the clearest example of what this book is ultimately inviting others to consider: that belonging is not something we do alone, but something we do together.

If I trace the line of my life, from the moment Marcela was placed in my arms, to the day I walked her out of the hospital, to the countless times I've defended her dignity, there is one truth that holds: The human spirit is not something you find. It is something you allow. It is the unmaking of who you were taught to be and the honoring of who you were meant to become. It is the first step into the unknown. The deep knowing beneath uncertainty. The love that becomes action. The vulnerability that becomes strength. The tenderness that becomes power.

It is the moment you open your hands, your chest, your life and say: I'm here. I'm willing. I'm no longer afraid to be me.

This is what Marcela gave me. Not in a grand moment of triumph, but in a quiet one—a single, trembling step into the light.

ᔓ

To belong, truly belong, requires more than proximity. It asks more of us than showing up or being allowed in. Belonging is not a chair offered at the edge of the room; it is the courage to be fully at the table. It demands intention, presence, and the fierce, ongoing practice of love. It is radical because it unsettles comfort. It disrupts the stories we inherit about who deserves space, whose bodies are credible, whose voices are legitimate, whose lives are deemed livable. Radical belonging does not wait to be invited. It does not soften itself into palatability. It insists: *I am here*, whole and unshrinking, and I make room for you to be here too.

Love, in this sense, is not a feeling that arrives unannounced or fades with ease. It is not tenderness without teeth. It is intention made of flesh, a disciplined choice, a daily act of will. Love is action shaped by attention. It is the deliberate refusal to let another's humanity be reduced, overlooked, or managed into silence. To belong radically is to carve openings where others see only walls, to imagine connection where systems have trained us to see threat. It is to resist the idea that sameness is safety, that obedience equals worth, that difference must be explained or corrected in order to be tolerated.

Belonging is not passive; it is kinetic. It requires alignment, the steady bringing together of heart, mind, and action. It asks us to remain when retreat would be easier, to stand in uncertainty without grasping for control, to bear witness without rushing to judgment. Radical belonging teaches us how to say no when compliance is expected, how to remain open when fear tempts us to close. It asks us to loosen our grip on inherited assumptions and to practice reverence for what we do not yet understand.

This kind of belonging builds a home not out of convenience or conformity, but out of care. It is constructed slowly, with attention, through ethical love and embodied presence. It is sustained not by agreement, but by commitment. It is not safe in the way the world defines safety, and it is never effortless. But it is alive.

Radical belonging is a form of freedom. It reminds us that connection does not emerge from sameness but from the courageous acknowledgment of difference. It invites us, again and again, to open ourselves wider than we thought possible, for our own becoming and for the becoming of others. It asks us to choose love not as an idea, but as a practice made visible. And in making that choice, we do not merely transform our communities; we ourselves are transformed.

Conclusion

What the Heart Knows

EVERYTHING I HAVE WRITTEN HERE began with Marcela.

Not as an idea, not as a case, not as a lesson, but as a love that undid me. Loving her required more than adaptation; it demanded heartfelt transformation. She asked of me what no training, no theory, no credential ever had: to unlearn what I had been taught about value, ability, independence, and success, and to relearn how to see without measuring, how to love without conditions, how to belong without permission.

Radical belonging became my methodology because it had to. There was no neutral ground from which to mother her. There was no distance that did not cost us something. Loving her was not abstract; it was daily, embodied, and intentional. It was the practice of insisting that Marcela did not need to be fixed or justified to be worthy. Love, in this way, became praxis. A discipline. A refusal. A way of organizing life around her humanity rather than around the world's discomfort with difference.

This book is, at its core, a public letter of love to my daughter. But it is also an act of restorative justice, an attempt to repair the harm caused by stories that narrow what counts as a good life, a valuable body, a meaningful future. Writing became a way of returning dignity to what is so often erased: interdependence, slowness, vulnerability, care. In loving Marcela openly and without apology, I push back against the systems that would render her invisible or conditional.

Along this journey, I had to reckon with myself, not only as a mother, but as an academic. I was trained to analyze, to categorize, to produce knowledge that sits at a safe distance from the body. But Marcela collapsed that distance. Some truths cannot be held at arm's length. They must be lived. Theories cracked open under the weight of love, and what emerged was not less rigorous, but more honest.

My hope for Marcela is not that the world will one day make room for her. It is that she will never doubt her right to take up space. That she will grow surrounded by people and structures that recognize her difference as generative, not limiting. That she will inherit a future widened by love that was practiced loudly, publicly, and without compromise.

∽

There are moments in life that announce themselves with thunder—rupture, diagnosis, birth, injustice, awakening. And then there are the quieter moments, the ones that nearly go unnoticed, but end up shaping everything that follows. This book has been an attempt to gather them all: the loud ones, the quiet ones, the ones that broke me open, and the ones that stitched me back together in ways I never could have imagined.

When Marcela was born, a version of me ended. What I didn't yet know was that she had arrived not only to be mothered by me, but to remake me. I thought motherhood would be a linear ascent toward certainty. Instead, it was an invitation to unlearn, and a summons to shed everything that stood between me and the truth. Marcela became my clearest mirror, reflecting the biases I didn't know I had, the fears I pretended not to carry, the tenderness I was afraid to claim. Through her, I learned that knowledge accumulated through achievement is nothing compared to wisdom rooted in lived experience. And that belonging is not given, it is forged.

The systems around us tried to define her from the moment she entered the world. They tried to define me, too. But something in me—something ancient, fierce, maternal, spiritual—refused. Maybe it was the intuition that guided me through the NICU, or the 0.8 mm that separated me from another version of life entirely. Maybe it was the doctor who looked me in the eyes and said, "Sometimes life has to slap you in the face so you finally wake up." Maybe it was the premonition my husband had—of the Virgin Mary placing her hand over the child I carried—whispering a truth we wouldn't understand until much later: She wasn't here to be ordinary. She was here to reveal what the world doesn't see, what love can do, what we become when we choose each other fully.

I didn't always recognize it. For years I believed I was the one teaching her—how to navigate the world, how to persevere, how to stand up for herself. But as time passed, I began to understand the gift I had been given: Marcela was teaching me how to see, with eyes unclouded by assumption, with a heart willing to be undone so it could be remade with integrity.

This book is the story of that remaking. It is the story of what it means to mother a child who forces you to confront the scaffolding of the world—and the scaffolding inside yourself. It is the story of discovering that love is not a feeling: It is a practice and a choice. It is the story of becoming.

None of this transformation was mine alone. It was co-authored, written in the sacred space between who Marcela was becoming and who I was allowed to become because of her. It was born in the pauses between medical sentences, in the tiny acts of rebellion in hospital hallways, in the 2 a.m. feedings, in the classrooms where she insisted on being seen, in the love letters that carried my voice when the world grew too loud.

And it was shaped, too, by illness, by the moment my oncologist told me how close I had come to another life entirely. Only 0.8 mm. The width of the space between what was and what could have been. That brush with mortality did not frighten me—it focused me. It made the noise of my former life impossible to return to. It showed me that clarity is not an intellectual achievement but a surrender—a willingness to listen to the truths carried in the body, the spirit, the lived experience.

I once thought wisdom lived in books, institutions, and accolades. Now I know it lives in the quiet places where love meets courage.

Marcela did not just make me a mother. She made me a witness, a learner, a seeker—a woman who understands that certainty is a myth, but meaning is a choice.

And so this book ends not with answers, but with an invitation: to see differently, to love intentionally, to listen deeply, to choose courage, and to honor the wisdom that reveals itself when we allow ourselves to be changed by one another.

This is the knowing that saved me. This is the knowing that made us. This is the knowing that we offer to you.

May it open the door to your own becoming.

Marcela, this love is my offering to you. It breathes beneath every page, lives in every refusal to look away, every choice to stay near what is true. Our souls found one another and chose this life together, not by accident, but with will, with purpose, with intention. You arrived and rearranged me, in the most delightful of ways. You taught me how to see without measuring, how to listen beneath language, how to love without bargaining or fear.

The only validation you will ever need lives within you. The world may try to name you, to narrow you, to tell you who you are allowed to be. It may meet you with misunderstanding or harm. But you carry an inner knowing that cannot be taken, an intelligence older than permission, a light that does not require approval. May you trust it. May you love yourself so fully that no cruelty can make a home in you, so tenderly and so fiercely that when you fall, you rise again, not by hardening, but by returning to yourself.

We have chosen difference as our teacher. We have chosen to interrogate what was inherited, to question what was handed down as truth, to refuse the stories that confuse conformity with worth. We chose love not as sentiment, but as intention. And as you grow, may your devotion to yourself become a force that reaches outward, toward justice, toward tenderness, toward a world more spacious because you are in it.

This is my promise to you: you belong—not someday, not conditionally, not by permission, but here, now, and always. And in that belonging, love begins again.

—Love always,
mommy

www.ingramcontent.com/pod-product-compliance
Lightning Source LLC
LaVergne TN
LVHW090610110826
845146LV00001B/332

* 9 7 9 8 9 9 5 2 2 7 1 0 6 *